ATTACK ON A MAORI PAH.

Frontispiece.
Frontispiece.

BUSH FIGHTING.

ILLUSTRATED BY

Remarkable Actions and Incidents

OF

THE MAORI WAR IN NEW ZEALAND.

BY

MAJOR-GENERAL SIR JAMES EDW. ALEXANDER,

K.C.L.S., F.R.S.E. ;

AUTHOR OF "A CAMPAIGN IN CAFFRELAND," "EXPLORATIONS IN
AFRICA AND AMERICA," ETC.

WITH A MAP, PLANS, AND WOODCUTS

The Naval & Military Press Ltd

Published by

The Naval & Military Press Ltd

Unit 5 Riverside, Brambleside
Bellbrook Industrial Estate
Uckfield, East Sussex
TN22 1QQ England

Tel: +44 (0)1825 749494

www.naval-military-press.com
www.nmarchive.com

BY PERMISSION,

MOST RESPECTFULLY INSCRIBED˙

TO

FIELD-MARSHAL

HIS ROYAL HIGHNESS THE DUKE OF CAMBRIDGE,

K.G., G.C.B., K.P., G.C.M.G.,

COMMANDING IN CHIEF,

By the AUTHOR.

" The British Army, under whatever system, must always be the army of Marlborough and Wellington. It will ever, when the occasion requires and permits, inscribe new glories on the tablets of history and maintain its imperishable renown."— *The Right Hon.* EDWARD CARDWELL, M.P., *Secretary of State for War.*

INTRODUCTION.

The incidents of the Maori War of 1860–61 were published by me some years ago. The events which occurred then, chiefly in the Taranaki, were very interesting, subsequent "actions and incidents" were sanguinary and exciting, and afford useful instruction in Bush Fighting. As no other military or naval man (though many were very well qualified to do so) had given a detailed account of the last operations in New Zealand, I undertook the task, for I thought that in justice to the forces engaged, Regulars and Colonials, soldiers and sailors, their gallant deeds, their labours and sufferings, should be recorded. Thus I have introduced the name of every officer, non-commissioned officer, or private sentinel, soldier, or seaman I could discover, who is mentioned in any dispatch or report of a creditable action. I was liberally allowed by the Military and Naval authorities free access to all the documents at the Horse Guards and Admiralty relating to the Maori War, in order to produce a correct and authentic narrative, which I trust this will be found to be.

J. E. A.

WESTERTON, BRIDGE OF ALLAN, N.B.,
    March 1, 1873.

CONTENTS.

CHAPTER I.

CHAPTER II.

CHAPTER III.

CHAPTER IV.

CHAPTER V.

CHAPTER VI.

CHAPTER VII.

CHAPTER XVI.

LIST OF ILLUSTRATIONS.

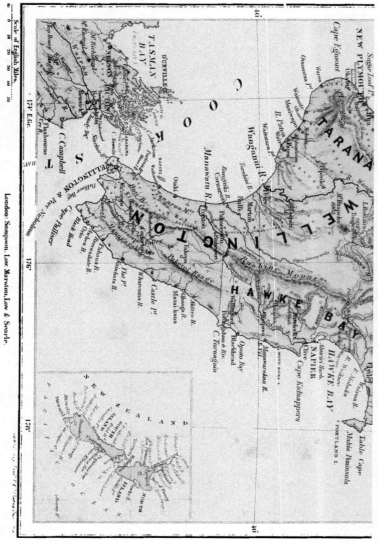

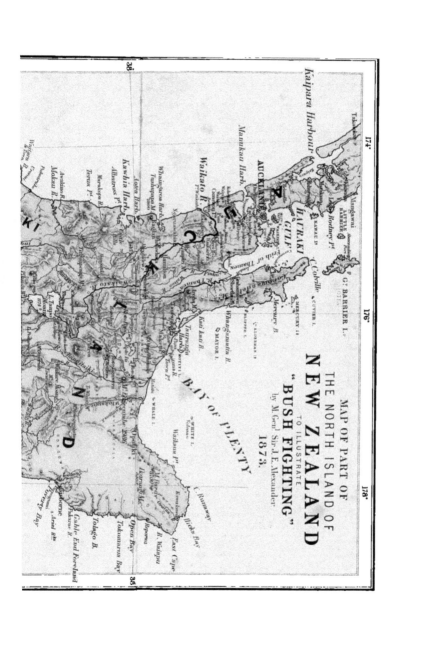

MAP OF PART OF
THE NORTH ISLAND OF
NEW ZEALAND
TO ILLUSTRATE
"BUSH FIGHTING"
by M. Gen.l Sir J. E. Alexander.
1873.

BUSH FIGHTING.

CHAPTER I.

Bush fighting, where practised—Qualifications for it—Equipment
of a Bush fighter—Head-dress, and how one should be shod
—Service in Africa, and in the American forest—Mounted
Riflemen — Americans appreciate them — Hants Mounted
Rifles—First experience in Bush fighting in the Andamans—
Mounted Rifles at the Cape—The Bush in New Brunswick—
A sketch of the Islands of New Zealand and the Maoris.

Bush fighting is a comprehensive term for warfare conducted in forests, in broken ground, and
on the hill-side. Wherever cover can be got, in
attack and defence, under the canopy of heaven,
there bush fighting can be practised, and it is
highly useful to practise it as a part of the army
manœuvres.

Of course, active and wiry men, of sound
constitutions, are best adapted for bush fighters.

B

Acuteness and intelligence are also wanted,
not heedless blundering, and needless exposure,
until the proper moment for the bold and fear-
less dash. The true bush fighter is content
with plain and wholesome fare, is very tempe-
rate in drink, or slakes his thirst, on service,
at the crystal spring, if stimulants are absent.
He is also not a slave of the narcotic pipe, and
thus is much more wide-awake than those who
are " blowing clouds " from " morn till dewy
eve," spoiling sight, and nerve, and appetite, and
good looks—the latter rather important for
young men who may wish to engage with a
nice partner, " battles over." The attitude of
a bush fighter, when near his enemy, is not a
dignified one, neither is that in deer-stalking
(which is an excellent preparation for rough
service in the field) ; he must stoop, and creep,
and take advantage of whatever cover presents
itself. A very clever medical man, Dr. Prothero
Smith, maintains (and he has excellent reason for
his theory) that for health and longevity one
should preserve the S or hollow in the back,

as long as possible ;—if this is not attended to, the bodily functions in front, those of the heart, liver, stomach, &c., are deranged and obstructed. This will be found to be perfectly true, on the least reflection, so after the object the bush fighter may have had in view, by stooping, &c., is accomplished, he should resume the elegant " Roman fall."

The equipment of a bush fighter is of great importance, loose, warm, serviceable clothing, nothing tight, or that would constrain action; head-dress light, and, if possible, sun and sabre-proof, and well ventilated. Before 1866 the German soldiers had a heavy helmet; they threw it away, and adopted a light and pleasant skull-cap as a helmet, and they retain it. For infantry, or mounted riflemen, the helmet (much more soldierlike than the shako) should be under a pound weight, with a light chain and ornaments, no spike, but a small, neat, " pine apple " or " acorn " knob at top.

The body to be clothed in a crimson Norfolk jacket, with inside pockets, and dark loose

trousers, boots 8 inches high, heels I inch,*
and leggings straight cut, and pulled on before
the boot, then pushed down over it, with a
light strap under the knee to prevent it shifting
round, and having no side buttons, as the boots
have no ties. Soles of boots 4 inches broad;
and if young men would consent to wear
straight-soled boots, they would find them to
last three times longer, and wear straighter and
more even than the usual kind, and look better
after several months' wear.

The above arrangements for the feet enable
a soldier to " shoe " himself, at a moment's
notice, and *in the dark;* a back loop helps
this, and no ties or buttons to trouble
him.

Red is our national colour, carries with it a
great *prestige,* and should, I think, be adopted by
our soldiers, of all kinds, as often as possible.
I had the honour at one time of holding a commission in the 16th (or " the Red ") Lancers ;

* This sort of short boot was found the best for shooting in
the Irish bogs, and was well tested.

and, on foot or mounted, I am very partial to "the red rag."

I was obliged to equip my men for the bush, in New Zealand, in blue "jumpers" (leaving the red tunics in store), because I could not get crimson flannel shirts. At 1000 yards, all colours are alike, as I proved ; red, grey, green, blue, black, all look hazy, except any man wearing a white cross belt, he becomes the target.

At the Cape of Good Hope we had leather trousers or "crackers" for the thorny bushes ; but these are not adapted for moist climates ; they do well in dry South Africa; also the veldt schoon, or field shoe of untanned hide, which the natives wear, and shift daily, have broad straight soles, and give no corns ; rather a comfort.

In Africa we had brown belts, no pipeclay, and long pouches to divide the weight of the ammunition round the waist, the pouch or pouches supported, if too heavy, with shoulder straps. The rifle was cased against damp. For months we slept on the ground, on skins, without a tent, but in rainy countries a pair of blankets supported by rifles, and four men inside with two other blankets ; and if waterproof sheets are added, it is a shelter not to be despised. One may be wet all day, as when we were employed exploring in the American forests ; but it would have been foolish, and one would not last long, if there was not a change to sleep dry at night ; and it was agreable in these woods to be lulled by the music of the breeze on the tops of the pine trees, and refreshed by their wholesome, turpentine smell.

For messes of half a dozen, a small iron pot and kettle, half a dozen tin plates, " tots," and pewter .poons (all having their own knives), might serve for the cooking apparatus.

Mounted riflemen are of great value in bush fighting, those who have seen them on service appreciate them highly. The mounted riflemen of our American cousins following some British infantry, and coming up with them in a wood (in the War of 1812), fatigued after a long march, attacked them at great advantage to the fresh rifles. This was a lesson not to be forgotten.

I could find no good manual on bush fighting; but this we know, that the people who have had most experience in it are the Americans. Some of their late operations in the bush were on a very large scale, and splendidly carried out; both sides being most expert in the use of the axe, and in bush work, entrenchment, and abattis, on the greatest scale; these were made in a surprisingly short space of time, and both held and attacked with the greatest tenacity.

Some of the accounts of them published at the time of their sanguinary distressing civil war, were most interesting.

I consider Colonel Bower's Corps of Hants Mounted Riflemen quite a pattern one. I saw a number of them at the Autumn Manœuvres of 1872, in low-crowned hats and feathers, grey loose coats, loose cords, Napoleon boots, rifles and swords; they seemed able to go at any place or ditch. Dismounted, and one holding three horses, to skirmish with great effect on foot.

What was objected to by some old officers

was carrying the rifle, when mounted, muzzle
up, in a Namaqua bucket in front of the right
knee, and not slung at the back. But I carried
my rifle in the same way in Africa: it is a
wonderful comfort on the march, and it can be
easily slung at the back on occasion. Colonel
Bower thinks it might pull a man off his horse
in galloping through thick cover, or in a fall
break a man's back, or get broken. Let both
ways be tried, and, as the Maoris say, "enough
of this."

Lieut.-Colonel Evelyn Wood, V.C., 90th
Light Infantry, who raised a cavalry corps in
India, has experience and good ideas of what
mounted riflemen should be; that is, mounted
infantry carried to a particular point, and
executing certain duties without delay.

Mounted men might be of three classes:
dragoons, broad-backed and stalwart, to charge
with an overpowering crash, or complete a
victory on a beaten foe; light cavalry, to reconnoitre and feel for the enemy, as the
Prussian Hulans did in the late war; and

mounted riflemen, never firing or fighting mounted, but dangerous on foot, as well-trained marksmen, and " aiding and abetting " the artillery.*

My first experience of bush fighting was under very peculiar circumstances, and in a strange locality, since rendered notorious by the cruel assassination of the deeply regretted Governor-General of India, Lord Mayo, in the Andaman Islands, in the Bay of Bengal.

I was a cornet of Dragoons (the 13th L.D.), and proceeding from Madras as a volunteer to the first Burman war. The transport in which I sailed, with a wing of the 45th Regiment, ran short of water, and I landed with the chief mate, a Malay coxswain, and six Lascars, to search for water on the Little Andaman Island. The boat, with a boat-keeper, was anchored off the shore, and we proceeded

---

* In the bush fighter's kit, besides his Bible, I would particularly recommend that he place a very useful and portable volume by a very distinguished officer—' The Soldier's Pocketbook for Field Service,' by Colonel Sir Garnet Wolseley, C.B., K.C.M.G., Assist. Adj.-General, Horse Guards.

along the beach, by the edge of the thick forest, in our search for a stream.

Presently black heads appeared in the bush; we made signs of drinking, and approached the wild-looking natives, a negro race supposed to be from an Arab slave ship wrecked here long ago. They immediately drew their arrows to their ears, and defied us to approach. I offered them handkerchiefs, the red cap of the coxswain, all in vain, no signs of peace. The mate stood by me and the brave Malay coxswain; the Lascars had all fled, and waded into the sea to get to the boat. We had no arms except a sword I carried, so it was resolved to return to the ship and get an armed party. This was done; Major Hilton gave some of his fine old corps, the Sherwood Foresters. We landed again; but a hut of the natives having been discovered by the soldiers inside the bush, and some of the fishing gear in it being pulled about, must have irritated the natives, for we had not proceeded far along the beach, till a rattling shower of arrows came among us,

wounding three men. We fell back in skirmishing order facing the bush, backs to the sea ; a
volley was delivered at the bush, and *as the
nearer we got to it the safer we were,* the bugle
sounded the advance, and we charged into the
bush. The natives immediately fled—little
active fellows they were ; we then found the
water, sat down to a meal, and the natives stole
on us and shot a man in the loins, and he died.
We kept the assailants off with men in the trees,
and, filling our casks, rowed off to the vessel.
I have much reason to be thankful to Divine
Providence for not having " a brief career" on
this occasion.

After this we saw some powder burnt in
Burma, on the Irrawaddy ; where else I smelt
the villanous saltpetre " in the open," I need
not here more particularly recapitulate. We
wanted " bush " in the Crimea for firewood,
but it was very hard to be got. At the Cape
of Good Hope there was plenty of bush fighting
in the first Caffre war ; there I saw mounted
riflemen working on foot like a pack of hounds ;

Hottentots, with keen eyes, and curious in spoor or tracks. Their double-barrelled carbines were disliked by the Caffres, they thought it was not fair fighting. Afterwards I fought in the bush with wild beasts for a living, while exploring and surveying for the Government in the interior of Africa. I made a narrow escape in the bush, on the banks of the Tagus at Santarem, in the civil war in Portugal. From wearing a white cap in the hot sun I became a target.

With Lieutenant Simmons, R.E. (now Lieut.-General Sir J. Lintorn A. Simmons, K.C.B., Governor of the Royal Military Academy), and Lieutenant Woods, 81st (now Major Woods), we attacked the bush of New Brunswick and Canada East with axes, and, with our three parties of lumbermen or woodsmen, hewed our way through it for 300 miles, to explore and survey a track for the military road, Quebec to Halifax.

As it I was never to have done with the bush, I was directed to go to New Zealand to assist in the Maori war, in 1860. Thus, in various

ways, I gained experience, sometimes pleasantly
and sometimes painfully, of "the bush."

New Zealand, where occurred the bush fighting it is intended to describe in this work,
though one of the last of the colonies of the
British Empire to be settled, may rise to be one
of the first in importance hereafter. It has
various and many advantages; the two large
islands, the North and the South Island, and
the smaller Stewart's Island, are in parallels of
latitude in the great Southern Ocean, where
health can be enjoyed in climates similar to
those of the British Isles, and longevity attained.

This favoured region of volcanic origin has a
very diversified surface, ridges of lofty moun-
tains and isolated peaks, many of them thou-
sands of feet in height—the grand Mount Cook
of the Southern Alps is 13,200 feet high.
Amongst these grand ranges are valleys filled
with everlasting glaciers, cascades, and on the
sea border deep fiords.

Magnificent forests of valuable timber clothe

the hill-sides, and extend into the valleys, where there is abundant fine land for pasture or tillage. The country is abundantly supplied with water, streams, and picturesque lakes. The burning mountain, Tongariro, sends its smoke banner over the waters of the great Taupo Lake; and the most extraordinary region of hot springs is east of it at the famous warm Lake Roto-mahana, and the white and pink Cascades of Te Tarata. Good harbours are round the coasts, and there is mineral wealth in gold, copper, iron, and coal.

The native inhabitants of New Zealand, the warlike Maoris, are a very fine race of men, of Malay origin, and who are supposed to have found their way to New Zealand in large canoes, and escaping from oppression and trouble in their own land 500 years ago.

The powerful, well-built brown men have well-developed heads, covered with thick wavy black hair, and the faces of the older Maoris are tattooed in circles; many of the younger ones, and the half-breeds, omit this ornamentation.

TE TARATA HOT SPRINGS.

To face page 14.

The older Maori women have the lower lip tattooed blue, and a little tattooing on the chin. Many of the younger ones omit this; have fine eyes, and a fascinating expression. I hope they will not adopt the fashion, dangerous for the hair lasting long, of drawing it back and depriving the features of their natural frame, the hair. Many of the people still wear flax mats, with tasteful borders of various patterns; others use blankets, shirts, and trousers, and stuff gowns. They look best in their native attire. I tried to introduce for the men the kilt and knickerbockers, instead of trousers, where I was stationed. Of course I did not venture to suggest changes in the ladies' costume.

The language of the Maoris is forcible and expressive, and not difficult to be acquired. They are fond of oratory, and introduce songs in their harangues; as to music, they are much impressed and touched with it. I am not aware that they have yet had the advantage of hearing the martial strains of the great Highland bagpipe, than which nothing is more exhilarating to march to, or the lively tap of the kettle drum and the spirit-stirring bugle.

Thirty or forty years ago the rough whalers and traders, who came from the North to the coasts of New Zealand, did not improve the manners and customs of the Maoris; firearms were introduced, native wars went on, and land was acquired from the natives by sometimes questionable means, leading afterwards to disputes and great trouble. Then the missionariés appeared on this field, and were of great service in the cause of civilization and religion; *they did their best,* and certainly put an end to cannibalism, which now it is a disgrace even to hint at. No doubt it originated in a craving for animal food where there were no wild animals to satisfy a raging hunger.

Missionary influence might always be well exercised in promoting the construction of better ventilated houses than the lowly and confined huts or wharrés of the natives, suggesting sanitary arrangements generally, and how to preserve health by self-control in various ways.

Merchants of high character and settlers, who would disdain to occupy native land improperly, have materially helped, and will assist in the work of native progress.

The Maoris are great agriculturists, and since the destruction of the gigantic race of birds, the Moas, 12 and 14 feet in height, and the want of objects of the chase, the Maoris were obliged to look to their mother earth for support. Potatoes, originally left by the great navigator Cook, form their staple food, and pigs, also Cook's gift. There are now wild cattle in the woods; pheasants introduced of late years are rapidly spreading in the islands; and game will probably be plentiful.

A beautiful and interesting publication by Dr. Walter Lawry Buller, F.L.S., &c., Resident Magistrate of Wanganui, gives the history of the birds of New Zealand, their appearance, and peculiarities. It was high time that a complete account should be given of the ornithology of New Zealand before any of the native species disappear or become very rare; and the in-

C

telligent author of that work has spared no
pains or trouble to produce it in a most attractive form.

The New Zealand quadrupeds consisted long
ago of a rat. In the lakes and rivers there are
only eels and a species of white-bait, but round
the coasts abundance of the finny tribes. Salmon
are attempted to be introduced. They require
a cold sea to resort to, and this can be got
off the South Island.

The Maoris have shown themselves not only
to be brave soldiers, but good whale fishers,
bold and active in boats. In the days of Cook
it is supposed they numbered 200,000 souls, and
now 40,000; the Europeans 200,000. As at
Natal, where some tribes under British protection do not diminish but increase, so might
the Maoris under good management and a wise
system.

New Zealand has been under British governors
since 1840. It was necessary to assume possession of it to check the lawless proceedings of
the rough white men of various nations, and

who required to be kept in check. His Excellency the Governor is assisted by a Legislative Council of forty. The House of Representatives consists of seventy-six members, four of whom are intelligent Maoris. The qualifications to vote for Representatives are paying a rent of 10*l.* in town, and 5*l.* in the country, or owning property of the value of 50*l.*

New Zealand is divided into nine provinces, for the purpose of local district government, viz., Auckland, Waikato, New Plymouth (or Taranaki), Nelson, Otago, Canterbury, Hawkes Bay, Southland, and Marlborough. I had the honour of commanding in the first of these—Auckland—for some time.

CHAPTER II.

The Tataraimaka block of land in Taranaki—Abandoned, and to
be reoccupied—Appropriation of the Waitara block the cause
of the previous war—Is now given up, yet the natives assume
the offensive by a deed of blood—A party of officers and
soldiers surprised by an ambuscade and slain—Preparations
for attacking the hostile natives—Their positions in strong
ground—General Cameron forms a corps of cavalry—Lieut.
Wallis's adventure—The troops march out of New Plymouth
to engage the enemy at Katikara—The transport service—
Dispositions for the attack of the enemy's position — The
details of the fight—Loss of the enemy, and their gallantry—
Their defeat—The troops thanked—The General returns to
Auckland to engage in another campaign in Waikato.

THE Tataraimaka block of land, twelve miles
south of New Plymouth, Taranaki, from which
the European settlers had been driven during
the previous contest with the Maoris, had been
retained by the natives as they said "by right
of conquest," and it was now determined to
reoccupy it.

The cause of the war of 1860–61 was the

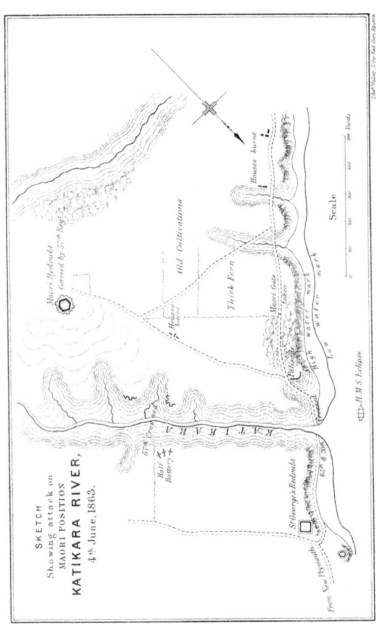

SKETCH
Showing attack on
MAORI POSITION
KATIKARA RIVER,
4th June, 1863.

From New Plymouth

St George's Redoubt

63rd & 70th

Half Battery

57th Crossed

KATIKARA

Maori Redoubt
Carried by 57th Reg.t

Houses burnt

Old Cultivations

Thick Fern

Maori Gate

Palisade

Pa tuka tuka taken

High water mark

Low water mark

Houses burnt

H.M.S Eclipse

H.M.S Eclipse

Scale

0   100   200   300   400   500 Yards

Edwd Weller Litho Red Lion Square

D.J Gamble

occupation of the block of land, one mile square, at the mouth of the Waitara, Taranaki, though a sum of money had been paid for it to an individual of the tribe, Taera, who alleged it was his, but the whole tribe claimed it. The chief of the tribe was Wuremu Kingi. The policy of the government of the colony was now to remove the chief cause of dissatisfaction on the part of the natives, and it was resolved to issue a proclamation to the effect that the Waitara block was to be given up.

Unfortunately before the proclamation was issued, the Tataraimaka block was occupied by the troops at St. George's Redoubt, the natives making no opposition. General Cameron had long before strongly advised that whilst negotiations were in progress for peace, the Tataraimaka block should be reoccupied as one of the preliminary conditions of peace; but this wise counsel was not followed.

In a letter to the War Office, of March 1862, General Cameron says, " Before leaving the Waitara, and while the bulk of the force (employed in the war of 1860-61) was still in the province of New Plymouth, I referred to the late Colonial Government the question of the occupation of the Tataraimaka block, which might at that moment have been carried out without opposition, as the natives had retired to their own districts. This course was not pursued at the time, and it is probable could not now be adopted without exciting a general war."

On the 4th of May, 1863, the natives assumed the offensive, marking their hostility by a very dark deed of blood; formerly they used to give warning of hostile intentions, but on this occasion they did not do so. Two officers, Lieutenant Tragett and Assistant-Surgeon Hope, were coming in from Tataraimaka to New Plymouth, and having reached a point on the sea beach (four and a half miles from Tataraimaka) where the Wairu* stream passes into the sea, were observed by an escort of six soldiers of the 57th Regiment with a prisoner, marching behind them, to stop. When the escort came up to the

* Turbulent water.

officers, the whole party were fired on by Maoris concealed behind a bank. The whole were shot and tomahawked except one man, private Kelly, who was wounded, but escaped; he crawled into the bush, and was found by a party who came to the relief from Tataraimaka.

Two bullock drays on their way to Tataraimaka, with stores from Poutoko* post (halfway to Tataraimaka from New Plymouth), were at the moment of the attack descending a hill to the Oakura river, accompanied by four drivers and an escort of a corporal and four men (too few in so dangerous a locality). They saw what had happened from about half a mile. The drays immediately turned to retire, and the party, pressed by the Maoris, were compelled to fall back, leaving the two drays, one of which (laden with flour and potatoes) the Maoris carried off with the team of bullocks belonging to it; the other was afterwards recovered, and brought back to Poutoko.

* A boundary stake; that is, a staff driven into the ground to mark a boundary.

A party of thirty men, under Captain Shortt, 57th Regiment, immediately proceeded from Poutoko to Wairu, and found the bodies of the officers and men. One body was not discovered until the 30th of May.

In consequence of this atrocity the Oakura (St. Andrew's) Redoubt was thrown up on high ground commanding the beach, at a point two miles south of Poutoko, and garrisoned by 150 men of the 57th Regiment.

The day before the massacre of the party just described, a report was brought into New Plymouth that an ambuscade was about to be laid; the report was not believed, but Captain Greaves, Deputy Assistant Quartermaster-General, was directed to go towards Tataraimaka to make observations. He did so, and as he approached the place where the party was afterwards destroyed, a Maori woman came out of the bush, and throwing her arms round the neck of Captain Greaves' horse, and pointing to the bush below, said, " No go!—bad man—no go !" This was at noon, when Maoris usually eat. A settler came along who had not been harmed, and Captain Greaves, seeing nothing, rode back to town. But the Maoris had, no doubt, been in the bush, and had merely retired for a short time. All praise is due to the Maori woman for her good intentions towards Captain Greaves.

His Excellency the Governor Sir George Grey, K.C.B., and General Cameron, C.B., Commanding the Forces, were at this time at New Plymouth, the military head-quarters not being yet removed from Auckland. It had been intended that the 65th Regiment should have embarked for England, and be relieved by the 2nd battalion of the 18th Royal Irish; but all moves were now suspended, and the Head-quarter Staff, 150 men of the 70th Regiment, and 100 of the 40th Regiment, with a quantity of entrenching tools, camp equipage, &c., were placed on board H.M.S. " Eclipse," for New Plymouth, where they were disembarked on the 10th of May.

The Maoris now were full of fight, and took up a strong position on the spurs of the Kaitaki

range, and about 4000 yards inland, facing the
sea. Their position was strengthened with rifle-
pits; they made signals at night by fires, and
during the day by pouring water on heated
stones, and the steam thus generated was seen
to a great distance.

Though the ground was in many places open
to the eye towards the Maori position, yet it was
intersected by deep gullies, covered with bush
and clothed with high fern, and in several
places with thick undergrowth.

The redoubts at Oakura and Poutoko were
square, 50 yards by 40, and flanked at opposite
angles by square projections or bastions.

To supply the want of cavalry, General
Cameron had decided on the employment of a
mounted force at Taranaki, and made arrangements for 100 men, under the command of a zealous and intelligent officer, Captain Mercer, R.A.,
being at once converted into a troop of cavalry,
as a temporary measure in this emergency.
Sabres, carbines, and revolvers were issued to
them.

OAKURA.

To face page 26.

In the first Caffre war (1835), at which I assisted, Sir Benjamin d'Urban mounted a very useful body of men in a similar manner from the 75th Regiment.

On the 29th of May, Lieutenant Wallis, 57th Regiment, when passing between Oakura and Poutoko redoubts, was fired on by a party of natives in ambush, half a mile out of Poutoko. His horse was shot through the head—one of the natives rushed to tomahawk Lieutenant Wallis; he fired his revolver, and the native fell, and the others made off. The wounded man was afterwards captured by a party under Colonel Warre, C.B., 57th Regiment.

It was on the left bank of the Katikara river that the natives had collected about 600 fighting men in a strong pah, and General Cameron determined on attacking their position and striking a decisive blow.

He accordingly marched out of New Plymouth on the night of the 3rd of June, with nearly the whole of the regular troops forming the garrison of the town, and proceeded towards the Katikara river. In order that the march might not be impeded, the guns, mortars, and reserve ammunition had been sent on a few hours before, under a strong escort, and no tents or baggage of any kind were allowed to accompany the column. The officers and men (dressed in dark blue serge tunics) carried each a blanket and a day's provisions in their haversacks, cooked. The weather was cool, and all were in good health, and in a mood to revenge their surprised and murdered comrades.

The column having been joined on the line of march by detachments of the 57th Regiment from the outposts, arrived at St. George's Redoubt a little before 4 o'clock on the morning of the 4th of June. The strength and composition of the force was as follows :—

General Staff, 5; Field officers, 5; Serjeant, 1.
Medical Staff, 2.
Commissariat Staff, 1.
Royal Artillery—Captain, 1; Subalterns, 3; Non-commissioned officers and men, 125.
Royal Engineers—Subalterns, 2; men, 13.
40th Regiment—1 man.
57th Regiment—Field officers, 2; Captains, 3; Subalterns, 8; Staff, 3; Non-commissioned officers and men, 380.

65th Regiment—Captain, 1; Subalterns, 2; Non-commissioned officers and men, 82.

70th Regiment—Field officer, 1; Captains, 3; Subalterns, 6; Staff, 1; Non-commissioned officers and men, 224.

Transport Corps—Captain, 1; Non-commissioned officers and men, 6.

Total, officers and men, 873.

Before leaving New Plymouth the General had arranged with Captain Mayne, R.N., that H.M.S. " Eclipse" should be at the mouth of the Katikara river before daybreak, ready to cooperate in the attack.

Colonel G. D. Gamble, the Deputy Quartermaster-General, to whose share fell all the arrangements for moving and camping the troops, remarked, as to transport, that the bullock-carts in the province of Taranaki could not be surpassed in suitability to the nature of the country. A light handy dray, capable of conveying half a ton, was drawn by four or even two bullocks; these carts kept up tolerably well with the ordinary pace of a column, and were, in fact, the only kind of transport which could be relied on for communication in New Zealand during the winter months, when deep ravines and rivers have to be crossed, and unmetalled roads, cut up by traffic and rain of tropical force, have to be traversed.

The Katikara river, which was the southern boundary of the Tataraimaka block, and divided European from native land, takes its rise in one of the ranges of Mount Egmont, that noble feature in the New Zealand landscape, its snow-capped peak 8270 feet high. The Katikara flows between steep banks of from 50 to 60 feet high, in a N.W. direction to the sea. The stream is rather rapid, average breadth 25 feet, except at its mouth, where it spreads out, and is only a foot and a half deep.

Besides this ford Mr. Bayley, a Tataraimaka settler, gave information of another 600 yards up the river, and giving easy access to the left bank.

About 600 yards from the upper ford, and S.E. of it, the Maoris had thrown up a palisaded earthwork or pah; this marked the right of his position, whilst his left rested on the flax bushes and the road near the beach.

To attack this position the general ordered
the following disposition of the force to be
made. The demi-battery, Royal Artillery, under
Captain Mercer (three Armstrong guns) moved
along the right (or north bank) of the Katikara
river about 500 yards, and unlimbered close to
its edge ; the 57th Regiment, under Colonel
Warre, took up a position in support of the
guns and to their left. The guns were to shell
the gullies, rifle-pits, and surface of the ground
on the opposite bank and plateau, so as to drive
the enemy from his cover, and were also to play
on the enemy's redoubt above alluded to, and
which appeared to be his strongest point.

Under this fire, combined with that of H.M.S.
" Eclipse," on board of which was his Excellency
the Governor (well acquainted with Maori warfare in 1846), the 57th Regiment was to cross
the stream at the upper ford, there two and a
half feet deep, and on descending the bank
throw out skirmishers to the front ; one division
to wheel to the right, sweep the plateau towards
the sea, clearing the enemy's rifle-pits at the

point of the bayonet, and turn up from the bend
of the road towards the pah : another division
was to show front towards the pah, with a view
of checking any movement from that direction,
after which the redoubt was to be carried by
assault, and an attack was also to be made on a
Kainga or native village, Tiki-tiki-papa, one
mile to the south.

All these arrangements were carried out in a
way that left nothing to be desired.

At a preconcerted signal the heavy guns of
H.M.S. " Eclipse " threw their shells (100-
pounder Armstrong and 8-inch) with good
effect into the enemy's position.   The 57th
advanced under Colonel Warre, C.B., in admirable style, under the accurate fire of Mercer's
Armstrongs, their right being covered by skirmishers of the 70th Regiment along the right
bank of the river ; the 57th ascended the
plateau, when they came on a sharp musketry
fire from the thick fern and from the rifle-pits
of the enemy, whom however they soon drove
in confusion before them.

The leading division, conducted by Colonel Warre, C.B., consisted of volunteers under Lieutenants Brutton, Waller, and Ensign Duncan; Brevet Lieut.-Colonel Logan commanded the supports.

While these movements were in progress, the 70th and detachment of the 65th Regiments were in reserve in rear of the St. George's Redoubt (which was near the beach, and 280 yards north of the mouth of the river), and were ready to move to any point at which they might be required.

As soon as the General perceived that the 57th Regiment were carrying everything before them towards the road and the sea, he led the reserve rapidly across the river's mouth, and ascended to the table-land without opposition; the enemy, having thrown up a mound, with a light palisading, had already fled with precipitation from that point. On reaching the high ground, the musketry and cheering announced that the 57th were assaulting the pah.

Lieutenants Brutton and Waller had wheeled

their parties to the right, extended, and turned the rifle-pits towards the sea so as to free the lower ford; they followed the enemy about a mile, inflicting loss on him, and burning the wharres or huts of the kainga or village.

Meanwhile Ensign Duncan had wheeled his party to the left, and, supported by the main body under Colonel Logan, pushed on towards the pah, strongly entrenched. The 57th were received by a heavy fire from the rifle-pits round the pah, but nothing daunted by the serious opposition and heavy fire of the enemy, Ensign Duncan pushed steadily forward, closely followed by the divisions under Captains Shortt and Rupell, under the immediate command of Colonel Logan, and supported by Captain Woodall and Lieutenant Thompson with the two remaining divisions.

In a few minutes the fire was returned, but finding it of no avail against an almost invisible foe concealed in rifle-pits, the whole rushed forward with the bayonet, and vied with each other in entering the position. Jumping over

the rifle-pits, from which they met with a most
determined opposition, the Maories fighting
desperately to the last, a hand-to-hand combat
ensued, which was terminated by the wharres
catching fire, and burning many of the defenders
in the ruins. Ensign Duncan and Captain
Shortt were the first to jump into the Maori
redoubt, followed by Privates I. Donaghy and
B. Stagpool, and the other officers and men.
The Maoris stood on the parapet to receive the
stormers, and were there bayoneted by the
men.

Twenty-one Maoris were taken out of the
rifle-pits killed, and seven were burnt in the
wharres, and many wounded were seen to
escape into the bush, after fighting with great
bravery.

The loss to the troops in this very dashing
and well-arranged conflict, was three men killed
and eight wounded.

The General was an eye-witness to the rapid
and regular manner in which each party performed the duties allotted to it. Of the personal

staff who on this occasion, and in previous
arrangements, were of the greatest assistance,
there were Lieut.-Colonel Gamble, Deputy
Quartermaster-General, Deputy Inspector-General of Hospitals Mouat, C.B., Lieut.-Colonel
Hutchings, acting military secretary, Major
M'Neil, A.D.C., Brevet-Major Paul, Brigade-
Major, Captain Gorton, 57th Regiment, extra
A.D.C. Colonel Whitmore, late military secretary, now settled in New Zealand, was also
present on this occasion.

Colonel Warre thanked Lieutenant and Adjutant Clarke for his zeal and energy, Ensign
Mace of the Taranaki Militia, Mr. R. Parris,
assistant native secretary, Quartermaster Mar-
tindale, Sergeant Cleary, and nine volunteers
of the 70th Regiment.

The wounded were taken on board the
"Eclipse" for New Plymouth, to which the
Lieutenant-General and staff, with 150 of the
troops, returned by the same opportunity, and
disembarked at 1 o'clock P.M. The remainder of
the troops marched back from Tataraimaka to

their respective posts, the New Plymouth portion arriving at their destination about 5 P.M., having within the twenty previous hours marched thirty miles, taken part in an action with the enemy, and twice forded four rivers by the way.

The whole force was in high spirits, marched splendidly to a man, and behaved throughout with the characteristic bearing of the British army.

Since the action at the Katikara, the southern natives, Taranakis and Ngateruanuis, were much disheartened with their defeat. Two principal chiefs fell that day, and the son of one of them afterwards tried to rally his father's followers round him.

They began to strengthen a position on the Kaitaki ranges, two miles from the sea, and midway between New Plymouth and Tataraimaka, with long rows of palisading, and flanked at intervals, besides a square pah or redoubt which commanded the approach.

The inhabitants of Taranaki province in the vicinity of New Plymouth were now obliged to come into town for safety, and the cattle were guarded at the pastures.

Colonel Gamble, accompanied by Captain Mercer, R.A., and directed by the Lieutenant-General, made a reconnaissance on the north bank of the Oakura river to select the most favourable position for shelling the enemy on the Kaitaki ranges. The natives yelled at the party from the south side of the Oakura river.

It was now found that the enterprising enemy, finding that their rifle-pits had been jumped over, covered them with a line of palisading, a space being left between the bottom of the palisades and the ground (except at intervals) to admit of the men firing on the ground level, after the usual way of defending pahs.

The weather being now very bad in the New Zealand winter, the shelling was deferred, and the General proceeded to Auckland to confer with his Excellency the Governor.

A letter came into New Plymouth from

Hapurona,* the fighting chief of the last war (of whom I made a sketch), challenging the troops to come out and fight " by the light of the sun."

By direction of the Lieutenant-General, Colonel Gamble now embarked in the "Eclipse" with 300 men, detachments of the 40th, 65th, and 70th Regiments, and proceeded to Auckland ; the head-quarters of the 18th Royal Irish now arrived—a very timely aid at this particular crisis, when trouble was expected in the Waikato. Colonel Warre remained at Taranaki as colonel on the staff, with 1500 men of the 65th and 70th Regiments and the militia.

The Waikato country—the expected scene of active operations—would combine the advantages of river communication with the benefit of a good road, at which the writer had lively recollections of labour for months when in command of the troops of the outposts of the Waikato.

Military telegraphs had also been judiciously established from Auckland in the direction of the Waikato.

* Absalom.

CHAPTER III.

Apprehensions of an attack on Auckland — Preparations for
carrying the war into the enemy's country — Disaffected
natives near the settlements — Murder of settlers — Boats
built for the Waikato—Colonel Wyatt's march to Tuakau—
Conversation with a Maori chief — The natives entrench
themselves in defiance of the troops—Lieut.-Colonel Austen
(14th Regt.) turns out his command and engages the enemy
on the heights of Koheroa—General Cameron gallantly leads
on to the rifle-pits—Difficult ground—The enemy defeated—
Their loss—Their arms—Captain Ring's convoy attacked in
the bush near Drury—Repulsed—Captain Ring attacks the
enemy at Kiri-kiri—Reinforced by Colonel Wyatt—Account
of him—Valuable services of the Navy—The "Avon" steamer
on the Waikato.

IN the end of June his Excellency the Governor
and the Minister for Native Affairs having
reason to believe that there was considerable
apprehension for the safety of Auckland from
the Waikatos (the most powerful and warlike
tribe in New Zealand), the Lieutenant-General
had collected as large a force as possible for its

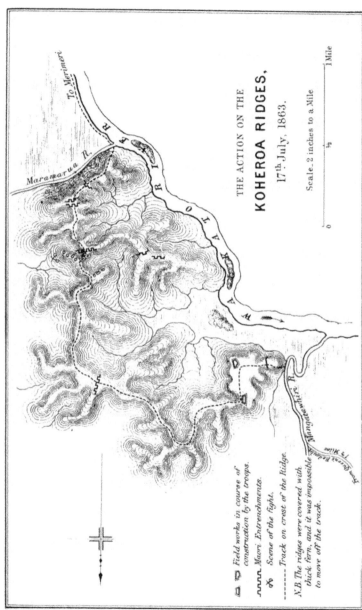

THE ACTION ON THE

KOHEROA RIDGES,

17th July, 1863.

Scale 2 inches to a Mile

▣ ◰ Field works in course of
construction by the troops.

ᴧᴧᴧ Maori Entrenchments.

⚔ Scene of the fight.

------ Track on crest of the Ridge.

N.B. The ridges were covered with
thick fern, and it was impossible
to move off the track.

To Merimeri

Maramarua R.

WAIKATO R.

Mangatawhiri R.

From River to Redoubt 1½ Miles.

protection, and to anticipate the design of the enemy by attacking them—"a bold initiative, often preventing a foe forming plans of attack, or carrying them into execution." Though the weather at this season of the year was unfavourable for operations in the field, yet, as it was almost certain from the information which had been received that the Waikatos, &c., would commence hostilities, it was thought better to take the initiative if possible, and carry the war into their country, than wait to be attacked at Auckland.

Reinforcements were expected from Australia in July.

Whilst preparations were being made for the expedition up the Waikato, information that the natives were about to rise and murder the out-settlers reached Sir George Grey, from so many quarters, that he considered it necessary that steps should be taken, without delay, to remove all disaffected natives from the vicinity of the European territory.

With this view, on the 9th of July, General

Cameron assembled a considerable force at Drury; while magistrates were sent round to the native villages with instructions to all of the inhabitants either to take the oath of allegiance, or to remove into the interior of the country. All refused the oath of allegiance (it was hardly expected they would take it), some deserted their villages, others had to be expelled by the troops, and the greater part, instead of removing into the interior, retreated into the bush between Drury and the Waikato, from which, on account of its extent and density, it was difficult to expel them.

They murdered and plundered several harmless settlers living near the bush. Among those who suffered for remaining on their farms was Mr. Meredith and his son, who, while working in the field, were tomahawked within a mile of Drury; near the same place Fahey, an old soldier of the 58th Regiment, and his wife, were murdered in the same manner. He was a true specimen of the military settler, and had made his homestead a perfect little Paradise, and, true to his military instincts, was ready to defend it against all comers.

The General established strong posts along the line of communication, and on the 12th of July he crossed, without opposition, the Mangatawhiri, and occupied the high ground beyond it with 400 men, an important position on the Koheroa range, to command the navigation of the Waikato river. The General also, with the assistance of Captain Sullivan commanding H.M.S. " Harrier," had boats built for the transport of provisions and stores up the Waikato, and it was also intended to bring a small steamer up the river to facilitate the operations in a district where they could look for no native supplies.

On the 12th of July 300 men of the 65th Regiment, under the command of Colonel Wyatt, C.B., marched from Drury, conducted by Captain Greaves, Deputy Assistant Quartermaster - General, by a bush track towards Tuakau, a native village on the right bank of the Waikato, eight miles below the Bluff

Stockade, near the mouth of the Mangatawhiri. The natives of Tuakau were disaffected, and a fort was established on high ground to command the passage of the river.

When the 2nd battalion of the 14th Regiment had the honour of being at the advanced outposts of the Waikato, near the Mangatawhiri river, with other troops under my command in 1862, a chief with whom I had friendly intercourse had told me "there is a Totara tree at the Mangatawhiri, which, if you cut it down, and make it a bridge and cross Hoeahs (soldiers) on it to Maori land there will be war ; if it is not cut down there will be peace." I said there was no intention of cutting it down, and I hoped that peace would continue.

The Waikatos having been active in hostility in the Taranaki, and also dangerous neighbours to the settlers near their own country, it had been resolved, as I stated, to move into the Waikato country. . This intention seemed to be well known to the Maoris, for on the 12th of July a large number of natives were observed from the 14th camp (which had now been formed on a commanding position east of the Mangatawhiri) to be entrenching themselves on the heights of Koheroa on the east side of the Mangatawhiri, apparently with the intention of obstructing a further advance up the Waikato.

Lieut.-Colonel Austen, 14th Regiment, an active and zealous officer, and much esteemed,* who was commanding on the spot, immediately called in all his working parties engaged on the South Road, &c., got his battalion under arms, and moved in skirmishing order against the enemy, followed by the detachments of the 12th and 70th Regiments, which were at the time arriving at the camp, as a reinforcement. The strength of the force was thus 553 officers and men.

Lieut.-Colonel Gamble, Deputy Quartermaster-General, who happened to be present superintending the encampment of the 12th and 70th Regiments, sent immediately a report of

* He succeeded me in command of the regiment.

what was occurring to General Cameron, who at once hastened across the Mangatawhiri, and overtook the troops during their advance.

When the troops came within musket shot of the enemy, he opened a sharp fire, to which the 14th skirmishers replied with such effect that the Maoris were soon compelled to retire, which they did slowly and without precipitation.

The advance was along a narrow track, which followed the curvature of open, tortuous fern ridges, the sides of which, in many places precipitous, fell into swamp. The tops of the ridges occasionally expanded into small table-lands of 100 and 200 yards in width, and again contracted into narrow necks and spurs, the whole forming a semicircle in front of the encampment.

The ground over which the enemy retired was thus most favourable for defence, as the only road by which the troops could advance against him led for about five miles over these very narrow fern ridges, the sides of which were too precipitous to admit of turning the enemy's position by a flank movement; and at several well-selected points, completely commanding the narrow tracks over which the troops were compelled to move to the attack, he had constructed lines of rifle-pits.

The strength of the enemy was estimated at about 400.

The rifle-pits were defended with great obstinacy, and as there was no artillery in the field, the enemy could only be dislodged with the bayonet, which was done with great gallantry by the young soldiers of the 14th Regiment, led by their commanding officer Colonel Austen, who received a severe wound in the arm during the action.

On coming within range, Captain Strange, 14th Regiment, with his company ran rapidly forward and occupied a ridge on the right of the enemy's retreat, the latter halting immediately under cover of the crest, and opening a sharp fire across the intervening gully on the skirmishers, who rapidly replied.

The main body followed the line of the

enemy's retreat, and on reaching a small knoll
within 100 yards of the second line of rifle-pits,
was received by a rattling volley, which by its
suddenness and severity for a moment checked
the young battalion. The enemy here stood
well, and kept up a heavy fire, but the General,
galloping to the front, gave the word to charge,
and led on, cap in hand. The men, led by their
officers, gallantly dashed on, and drove the
enemy in confusion before them.

As the troops advanced the Maoris, running
in dismay to the nearest cover, sprang into a
ravine to their right. At this juncture the
troops, having formed round the semicircle of
high ground which embraced the ravine, poured
in a murderous converging fire on the enemy,
as he fled through the bottom of it.

Many of them here fell, others again keeping
on the high ground retreated to a further ridge,
where they again opened fire on the advancing
force. The troops again drove them from their
vantage-ground, and at length, broken and disheartened, they fled to the Mara-marua, a tributary

of the Waikato, which some crossed in canoes
and others by swimming.

The engagement at Koheroa commenced at
11, and ended at 1 o'clock. The enemy, in point
of ground and knowledge of it, had every
advantage, of which he availed himself with
remarkable intelligence and dexterity; and it
was a matter of congratulation that, for the
first time in the annals of New Zealand warfare,
he was defeated in fair combat on open ground
without artillery, to the presence of which alone
in former wars he attributed the British supe-
riority.

It seems singular that the Maoris, with all
their native pluck and activity, had not provided
themselves with bayonets or substitutes for
them for close combat. It is true they had the
flat meree of stone or whale blade-bone and
tomahawks, but no swords or bayonets for a
charge, or to give confidence after a discharge
of fire-arms.

The enemy's loss, always difficult to ascertain
with certainty, could not have been less than

E

thirty or forty killed, besides wounded, of whom
he subsequently acknowledged to have had a very
heavy list.

Immediately after the action twenty bodies were
counted, more were found next day, and there
were marks of others having been meanwhile
removed. The casualties of the troops were
two men killed, one officer (Lieut.-Colonel
Austen) and ten men wounded. The enemy
threw away their arms, ammunition, food, and
clothing to facilitate their escape : this is not
unusual in defeats generally. In each of their
haversacks or bags was found a three days'
supply of damper (flour cakes), and one of the
gospels or a Church of England prayer-book in
the Maori language, showing that they had
once been under the influence of Bishop Selwyn.
The slain Maoris were all very fine-looking
men, whom one could not help regretting.
They seemed Waikato rangatera, or gentlemen.

General Cameron spoke highly of the conduct
of the officers and men engaged at Koheroa, and
of the able manner in which the troops were

led by their commanding officers, viz.: Lieut.-
Colonel Austen, 14th, Major Ryan, 70th,
and Major Miller, 12th. Among the officers
who had the good fortune to have the opportunity of distinguishing themselves by
conspicuous forwardness in the attack were
Captain Strange, 14th (afterwards a Major),
who did good service with the advanced skirmishers ; Captain Phelps, who led his company
to the charge ; Lieutenants Armstrong, Glancy,
and Ensign Green, 14th. Surgeon-Major Carte,
M.B., 2—14th, attended to the wounded under
fire, and obtained the C.B. Colonel Mould,
C.B., R.E., was also present, and Colonel Gam-
bier, Major M'Neil, A.D.C., and Lieutenant St.
Hill, extra A.D.C., actively assisted on the staff
of the General.

It was suggested about this time that a
European regiment, or a regiment of Sikhs,
should be sent from India to reinforce the troops
in New Zealand, but this was not carried into
effect.

A convoy and escort returning from the

Queen's Redoubt, Waikato river, to Drury, under Captain Ring of the 18th Regiment, was attacked on the 17th of July by a party of natives in ambush, at a place called, during the road-making operations of 1862, the "Stone Depot," about four miles from Drury.

The enemy, three times the strength of the escort, as was afterwards ascertained, had taken post in the dense bush, which came up close to both sides of the road, and after the head of the convoy had passed, fired a volley into the centre of it from their concealment.

The horses of one of the carts fell, and the cart to which they were harnessed thus blocking up the road-way, divided the party. The Maoris rushed on the road, and attempted to overcome each party in detail. Captain Ring having withdrawn his men a short distance, charged the enemy with the bayonet, and drove him into the bush.

Finally, the enemy attempted to surround Captain Ring's party, of one subaltern, two sergeants, and forty-seven rank and file, and obliged him to retire to Martin the settler's house, which he occupied until reinforced—the casualties amounted to four privates killed, and ten officers and men wounded,

The conduct of Ensign Bricknell and that of the men was admirable, under most trying circumstances.

Again on the 22nd July, Captain Ring, at his camp near Kiri-kiri, hearing that two settlers had been fired on by a party of natives, and that one of the settlers was killed, and hearing firing at about two miles from his camp, proceeded there with about 100 men of his detachment and fell in with natives, who were engaged with sixteen volunteers. Fire was opened, and the natives retreated for a time, but rallying, were surrounding the detachment, which lost a man, the natives securing his rifle and bayonet. Captain Ring, knowing that the 65th were not far off, sent an artillery officer, Veterinary Surgeon Anderson, who gallantly vounteered his services, to render assistance, by bringing up a party by a track in the enemy's rear. Colonel Wyatt immediately got a party under arms, and proceeded to where he heard the firing and shouting, and at a turn of the path he suddenly came upon the combatants, the 18th men on an entrenched knoll, and the natives on level ground, but pressing them hard on three sides. The regimental call of the 65th and the "fire" was now sounded by Lieutenant Pennefather, which was answered by the 18th with a loud cheer. A rapid and continuous fire was now opened on the natives, ensconced in the gullies and sheltered by trees, from the fire of the 18th.

The Maories thus being taken by surprise from this timely succour to the 18th, after a smart action of ten minutes, fled toward the dense bush, and darkness now set in, but not before several natives had been seen to fall. The casualties among the troops amounted to one man of the 18th killed and four wounded, one 65th killed.

The officers and men under the trying circumstances to which they were exposed behaved admirably, including a detachment of Auckland Militia.

The officers named as having distinguished themselves at this skirmish at Kiri-kiri, were Lieutenant Wrey and Ensigns Jackson and Butts, 18th Royal Irish, Lieutenant Rait, R.A., Captain Gresson, Lieutenant and Adjutant Lewis, and Lieutenant Pennefather of the 65th, and Ensign J. B. Hayes, Auckland Militia.

Colonel Wyatt, now deceased, was a rough and ready soldier, and had been in the Royal Navy, and was always " full of fight," and enjoyed the excitement of it—just the man for a bush campaign—and liked also to sing a song, and join in a glass of grog, " merry in camp " after a day's work,—

> " When at night with victory crowned,
> Around the fires upon the battle ground
> We bivouac.
> Released from fighting, then we sink to rest;
> The ground our bed, tho' hard, it is the best
> That we can get.
> We laugh and sing, tho' ready are for duty,
> Smoke our cigar, and dream of home and beauty.
> O vive l'amour, cigars and cognac,' &c.

The Royal Navy now came into play with excellent effect, as they had done, as I related in the campaign of 1860–61, always ready to drag guns into position, to fire them, and engage at close quarters with pistol and cutlass. In the old Burman war of 1825–26, none so active, as we recollect, over the stockades as the blue-jackets, and here too at the Maori pahs.

The success of the troops in 1863 in New Zealand was owing in a great measure to the valuable assistance rendered by Captain Sulli-van, senior naval officer, and the officers and men under his command. A large party of seamen and marines of H.M.S. "Harrier" en-camped on the bank of the Mangatawhiri river since the 11th of July, and their services were of the greatest advantage to the land force, all the boats employed in conveying troops and supplies across to the Koheroa having been entirely manned by them.

At the request of General Cameron Captain Sullivan superintended the construction of six large flat-bottomed boats, especially adapted for the transport of troops up the Waikato. Two of these were brought overland from Auckland, a distance of thirty-five miles, to the Mangatawhiri, where they were extremely useful.

Without the aid of such boats operations up the Waikato could not have been carried on, as there was no road on either bank of the river.

The small colonial steamer "Avon" was brought into the Waikato from the Manukau harbour, West Coast, by Commander Mayne, H.M.S. "Eclipse," and was anchored off the Bluff Stockade at Havelock.

Captain Mayne derived great assistance from Captain Greaves, 70th Regiment, D. A. Quartermaster - General, a very zealous and intelligent officer, who had surveyed the lower part of the Waikato the previous summer, and now sounded ahead of the "Avon" and showed the channel.

The "Avon" could carry 200 men—her bulwarks were made bullet-proof and she was armed with a 12-pounder Armstrong gun.

CHAPTER IV.

March on Paparoa and Paparata—The New Zealand Bush—
Cleared along the Great South Road—A party of woodcutters
surprised, and lose their rifles—Ensign Dawson's skirmish—
The enemy takes up a strong position and fortifies it at Meri-
meri—The chief Wuremu Tamehana—The enemy's position
reconnoitred—The Maoris attack and plunder the Cameron
post—Captain Swift's party—Engages the enemy—Captain
Swift killed and Lieut. Butler wounded—Gallant and skilful
conduct of Colour-Serjeant McKenna — Non-commissioned
officers and soldiers who distinguished themselves—Forest
Rangers engaged—Major Lyons and Captain Inman's parties
engage natives plundering the settlers.

GENERAL CAMERON having been informed
that a body of the enemy had collected at the
villages of Paparoa* and Paparata† (about fourteen miles to the east of Koheroa position), he
marched from the Queen's Redoubt a force of
700 men, soldiers, seamen, and marines there,
on the night of the 1st of August—Captain
Sullivan, of H.M.S. "Harrier," accompanying

* Broad plains.　　　　　　† Rata, covered ground.

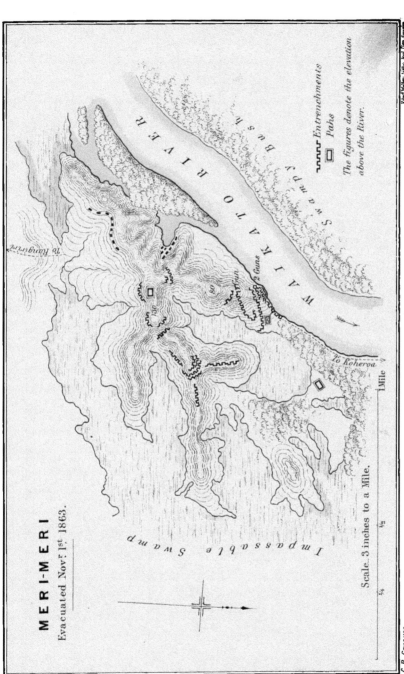

MERI-MERI

Evacuated Nov.r 1.st 1863.

Entrenchments
Pahs

The figures denote the elevation
above the River.

WAIKATO RIVER

Swampy Bush

To Paparata

2 Guns

80

130

To Koheroa

Impassable Swamp

Scale. 3 inches to a Mile.

1 Mile

1/2

1/4

Published by Longmans, Green, Reader, and Dyer, & Charles Knox, Buildings, 189 Fleet Street, London.

Edw.d Weller, Litho, Red Lion Square.

G. R. Greaves.

the force—with the intention of surprising them ;
but on reaching the villages they were found
deserted, the natives having retired into the
dense bush behind them, from whence they
wounded a soldier of the 12th Regiment. The
troops returned to the Queen's Redoubt about
3 in the afternoon, having been under arms
since 7 o'clock on the previous evening, and
having cheerfully marched about thirty miles.

The bush of New Zealand is wonderfully
dense and entangled. A European going into
it about twenty yards, and turning round three
times, is quite at a loss to find his way out
again, unless he is somewhat of an Indian
pathfinder, and can judge of the points of the
compass by the bark of the trees, the sun,
&c. Trying to run through the bush, one
is tripped up by the supplejack and other
creepers. " Why don't they follow the enemy
through the bush?" cries some one from an
easy-chair at home. Well, the troops always
did their best, at much damage sometimes to
their shirts, trousers, and skins. It was not

the custom here, as we used to do at the Cape
of Good Hope, to wear leather trousers, com-
monly called "crackers"—a great protection
against thorns, but, as I said, unsuited for moist
climates.

The Hunua forest, between Drury and the
Waikato, is a particularly dense "bush;" and
after what had happened to Captain Ring's
party, on the representation of General Cameron,
the Colonial Government had taken steps for
clearing the thick bush skirting the road between Drury and the Queen's Redoubt, and the
work was commenced by contract. The principle followed at first was, by way of experi-
ment, to clear the undergrowth of thick stuff
and saplings, with a view of burning them
after a few weeks, in piles, round the large
forest trees, which were left standing to be
killed by the effect of the fire.

It was believed that, while the labour of
clearing would thus be materially lessened, the
enemy would be deprived of thick cover, while,
should he attempt to avail himself of that

offered by the standing trees, there would be avenues made for following him. On the other hand, the large trees, if felled, would still afford cover for the enemy's ambuscades, and be, in the first instance, a serious obstacle to the troops in attempting to follow him.

On service, we all know that when a judicious order is given it should be most carefully obeyed. Thus General Cameron had directed that all working parties should have a covering party for protection near them ; but on August the 25th this precaution was not taken by a party of one sergeant and twenty-five men of the 40th Regiment, who were employed as bush cutters on the Great South Road, and were at work about half a mile from a similar party of the 65th Regiment.

The men had piled their arms at the edge of the bush near the road under the charge of a single sentry ; the enemy came stealthily through the bush and partial clearing over-grown with fern, at the opposite side of the road, drove in three or four civilian bushmen, and before the party of the 40th had time to stand to their arms, they rushed (after receiving the fire of the sentry) and seized the whole of the rifles, with the exception of three stand.

While the men were running to fall in, two were shot dead, and the remainder, seeing the arms lost, and that the enemy were getting round them, fell back into the bush.

Fortunately at this moment the advance guard of the regular convoy coming from Drury appeared in sight, and they, with the escort under Captain Cook, 40th Regiment, engaged the enemy, who, it proved, from the extent of the fire, systematically occupied the line of road in force. A sharp skirmish ensued, which lasted more than an hour, the troops being chiefly in skirmishing order along the road, and under the cover afforded by a cutting. The enemy numbered about 160 or 200; one of them was killed, and his body found; five or six others were seen to fall, but were removed. A man of the 18th Regiment was wounded.

The officers, who did good service on this

occasion under Captain Cook, were Captain
Ord, 65th Regiment, Captain Bishop, 18th
Regiment, Lieutenant Warren, 65th, Lieutenant
Thacker, 18th, Lieutenant Clark, Madras Cavalry
(a volunteer attached to the Transport Corps),
Lieutenant Pagan, 65th, and Ensign Haines,
18th. All the officers and men behaved ex-
tremely well.

The enemy had evidently laid his plans for
some time, and came solely with a view of
securing the arms. Colonel Gamble visited the
scene of attack the next day, and arranged with
the contractors that the whole of the axe-men,
soldiers and civilians, should work together, and
be protected by a covering party of forty men, to
be furnished from the two nearest military posts.

General Cameron's head-quarters being at
the Queen's Redoubt, the head-quarters of the
14th Regiment, under Colonel Austen (who
had recovered from his wound), with 100 men
of the 12th Regiment, were pushed forward to
Whangamarino,* overlooking the Waikato river,

* Placid river.

and in sight of the strong Maori position of Meri-meri. A strong stockade was erected by the troops under the direction of a popular and able officer, Captain Brook, R.E.; two 40-pounder Armstrongs were placed in position here, and in charge of Lieutenant Pickard, R.A., who did not fail to use them against the Maori works.

Single natives used to pay the troops daily visits at Whangamarino in the most daring manner—to have a shot at the sentries. One night the camp was alarmed by a sentry of the 12th Regiment, who had been attacked by a Maori on his post, and who attempted to seize the sentry's rifle with one hand and to tomahawk him with the other; he cut off the sentry's thumb, but did not get his rifle, and escaped uninjured into the forest.

About this time an Englishman made his escape from the Maoris by swimming the Waikato river. He had been in the Bengal Artillery; he was up the country when the war broke out, and was detained by the natives

and forced to teach them how to load and fire
the ship guns they had in position at Meri-
meri. To imitate the Pakeha, they used to
fire off a gun at tattoo, and call " All's well,"
and made a horn of native flax to imitate the
bugle-calls.

One day several large canoes were seen
coming down the river from Meri-meri with
a white flag flying. On being detained at
Colonel Austen's post, they were found to
contain a large quantity of potatoes and several
milch goats, as a present for General Cameron
and his soldiers, as the chiefs at Meri-meri had
heard that the General and his troops were
short of provisions, and in obedience to the
Scriptural injunction, " If thine enemy hunger,
give him meat; if he thirst, give him drink."
So the chiefs had sent their presents.

On the 25th of September, Ensign Dawson,
18th, was subaltern in charge of the Pokino *
picket, consisting of two sergeants and sixty
rank and file. They left the Queen's Redoubt

* Bad night.

F

about 7 o'clock A.M., and when within half a
mile of the Pokino village, he was attacked
in the rear by a body of Maoris.   Ensign
Dawson gave the word to face about and charge
the enemy, and they were driven down a gully
towards a swamp on the right of Pokino, and
were then followed for half a mile along a track
towards Paparoa. Hearing yells in the direction
of Pokino, the party returned along the track
to the open ground near the village, and on
arriving there they were received with a volley
from the enemy, who were extended across the
whole of the clearing, and were in the bush on
the right.   The men were perfectly steady
(before an enemy which appeared in great
force), remaining in skirmishing order, and
keeping up a steady fire, taking advantage of
any cover the ground afforded.   From the
commotion occasionally perceived among the
Maoris, the fire of the troops seemed effectual,
and the Maoris were removing their wounded.

Captain the Hon. F. L. P. Trench, 40th
Regiment, being ordered to move the inlying

picket to the support of the picket at Pokino village, when within half a mile of it he found the patrol under Ensign Dawson engaged with the enemy, who were firing from behind fallen timber. Captain Trench immediately reinforced the skirmishers, who advanced, drove the Maoris from the clearing and out of the village into the bush, Captain Noblett, 18th, joining in this affair. In scouring the bush two flint guns and some ammunition were picked up.

Besides Ensign Dawson, who had behaved in a most spirited manner before very superior numbers of the enemy, the names of Ensign Spiller, 65th, Ensign Gomez, 40th, and Lieutenant Croft, 18th, were brought to the notice of the General for zealous services.

A greater clearing than was at first intended was made along the Great South Road; all trees exceeding two and a half feet in diameter were cut down, and, with the assistance of 100 Nova Scotians, and some German colonists, a breadth was cleared of 220 yards on each side of this important road, so that a passage could be found for a horse through the remaining stumps and unconsumed logs.

There had been repeated reports of the intention of the enemy to return to the fighting-ground at Koheroa, but instead of that they took up a strong position higher up the Waikato, at Meri-meri native settlement. From the numbers observed to be engaged in the works there, and their industry in executing them, a determined resistance was evidently intended.

The general position of the enemy was on a high commanding slope on the right bank, looking directly over a reach of the Waikato. On this slope they had made a continuous double line of rifle-pits, running immediately across the track leading from the north to Meri-meri. This track has the great swamp of the Whangamarino, or Mara-marua river, on its left going south; after the swamp the track passes through a thick bush of Ti-tree, &c.

Low down, and near the water level, and in front of their main line of rifle-pits, they had cleared a large space of Ti-tree and scrub, and thrown up an earthwork as a position for two ships' guns, which they had had for years in their possession.

The intelligent chief, Wiremu Tamehana, called by the missionaries William Thompson,* commanded the Maoris here, who numbered about 1100 men.

The difficulty of carrying the position by assault could only be lessened by a covering artillery fire; and so four cargo-boats were purchased at Auckland, fitted for the reception of Armstrong guns with their carriages, so as to form floating batteries, and at the same time to transport the guns in a state ready for landing at any point.

The General and Colonel Gamble, to reconnoitre the enemy's position, proceeded in the steamer "Avon" on the 12th of August. Shells and rockets were thrown into the enemy's works, inflicting some loss. The enemy appeared in

* He was called the king-maker, for, to unite the tribes against the Pakeha (or white men) he had instituted a Maori king.

great numbers at their various works, and after each discharge from the " Avon," showed themselves along the line. On concluding the reconnaissance, when the steamer weighed to return, a running fire was opened on the " Avon " from the bush and flax, and was replied to by the rifles of the " Avon." One seaman was grazed with a buck shot.

The 14th Regiment's head-quarters had been advanced to the mouth of the Whangamarino, and occupied a new stockade there.

On the Waikato were two friendly chiefs, Kukutai and Te Wheoro, and provisions were brought up the Waikato in canoes manned by friendly natives. At a post called " Cameron" commissariat supplies had been stored under the protection of Kukutai's people—*en route* to the Mangatawhiri for the Queen's Redoubt. The hostile natives, with a force of 200 men, attacked Cameron on the 7th of September, took the place from Kukutai's people, and destroyed the commissariat supplies, consisting principally of bran, oats, and maize, and set fire to the pah.

Mr. Armytage, a district magistrate employed under the Native department of the Government, resided at Cameron in charge of the arrangements for canoe transport, had just reached the place before the attack, and was killed by the enemy.

The attack having been observed from the post at Tuakau, about seven miles higher up the Waikato, Captain Swift, 65th Regiment, commanding there, immediately started with one officer and fifty men in support of the friendly pah.

The route lay over a very difficult and circuitous bush track of about eight miles inland from the river. On coming near the place Maoris were heard through the thick bush speaking, and were at first believed to be approaching the party, who prepared to receive them. The enemy, however, not having come towards them, Colour-Sergeant McKenna volunteered to act as scout, and went forward alone to gain intelligence, and heard the Maoris conversing, and believed from their tone and manner that they were partly intoxicated.

Captain Swift then directed the men to fix bayonets and charge into an open space, where the enemy were really on the *qui vive*, and awaiting them. As our men, led by their officers, came to the clearing, they received a close volley in front, and on the left flank; Captain Swift fell mortally wounded, but directed Lieutenant Butler, the only other officer, to charge the enemy. As this officer was leading the men on, he, too, received a severe wound across the abdomen, after which he shot two Maories with his revolver. Colour-Sergeant McKenna then assumed the command of the party, which he handled, as Lieutenant Butler stated, with admirable coolness and skill.

It should be stated that while Captain Swift was moving to the post, his advance guard of twelve men missed the track, and in consequence of the density of the bush got separated from the main body, which they were never again able to rejoin, although they too were, during a part of the time, engaged with the enemy. Thus the party who met the first and most fatal

fire of the enemy only numbered thirty-eight;
these were further reduced by the number bearing the wounded to about thirty, and yet this
handful of men, after both their officers were
suddenly struck down, gallantly held their own
in the presence of 200 of the enemy, who did
not attempt to pursue them.

Captain Swift, before he left his post, had
judiciously sent a report to head-quarters at the
Queen's Redoubt, that he was about to start for
the relief of Cameron, when the General at once
decided on despatching from the Queen's Redoubt
150 men of the 65th, under Colonel Murray, in
support.

When Captain Swift fell mortally wounded,
after speaking a few words to Sergeant McKenna,
he handed him his revolver, and told him to lead
on the men after the fall of Lieutenant Butler.
The sergeant and his men now charged the
enemy furiously to revenge the fall of their
officers. Men in charge of Captain Swift and
Lieutenant Butler were sent to the rear, and the
body of a slain soldier was covered and con-

cealed with fern. The sergeant being on an open clearing, and greatly outnumbered, determined to hold his own till dark, hoping that the men in charge of Captain Swift and Lieutenant Butler, with two wounded men, would get well to the rear, and would be joined by the advance guard.

About 6 o'clock the enemy had worked round to the rear of the party, and thus cut off their retreat by the way they came. The sergeant immediately ordered a charge, and was met by a volley, which killed one and wounded three men. He now determined to retreat down the hill, which was covered with fern, and, sending on the wounded, he threw out a line of skirmishers, with the order, " Fire, and retire."

In this way they retreated down the hill in a steady, orderly manner, the natives coming out of the bush and firing at the party, but without effect on the men in motion. At this time it was near dark, and scrambling through the bush they lost the track, when the sergeant, calling his men about him, told them he should stay where he was until morning, and ordered that not a word should be spoken nor a pipe be lighted.

It was now found that four of the men were missing, but it was hoped they would turn up from the bush before morning. About five next morning the sergeant tried to regain the track out of the bush, and succeeded, and at 8 o'clock they were met half-way from Tuakau by Colonel Murray and his party, and regained the camp at 11 A.M. completely exhausted.

Acts of daring and gallantry like the above are sure to be appreciated, and deserve especial record ; and Colonel Wyatt, C.B., recommended to General Cameron Colour-Sergeant McKenna for some special mark of approval on the part of Her Majesty, who, after both his officers had been shot, charged through an enemy heavily outnumbering him, and drew off his party through a broken and rugged country with small loss.*

* He was most deservedly rewarded with a commission and the Victoria Cross.

The casualties in this affair were one officer (Captain Swift) and three men killed, Lieutenant Butler and four men wounded. Captain Swift was one of the best officers in the 65th; and Lieutenant Butler, in the previous Maori war, had always proved himself to be a valuable officer.

Lance-Corporal Ryan and privates Bulford and Talbot removed their dying captain from the field of action, and remained with the body all night in a bush surrounded by the enemy. Privates Thomas and Cole remained all night in the fern with Lieutenant Butler, and carried him in their arms in the morning towards the camp of the 65th, until assisted by Colonel Murray's party.

Drummer Welsh deserves especial notice, who, when private Grace was killed, picked up his rifle, and emptied his pouch of ammunition and copper caps, under a galling fire, and thus prevented the enemy obtaining that trophy.

Sergeants Bracegurdle and Meara did good service during this desperate affair. As to the enemy's loss, Colour-Sergeant McKenna stated he believed between twenty and thirty of the enemy fell, killed or wounded; seven he saw shot dead, and dragged into the bush.

After I had the honour of being directed by H.R.H. the Duke of Cambridge to raise the 2nd Battalion, 14th Regiment, in a private conversation with that noble officer—the late Field-Marshal Lord Seaton, in Dublin—he said, "We cannot too highly esteem that valuable body of men—the non-commissioned officers of the British army." And thus, as an old soldier, I take pleasure in recording their gallant conduct at all times, as well as that of the brave private sentinel.

On the same day with the above (7th September), a skirmish took place between a party of natives and thirty men of the Forest Rangers (a body of settlers) under Lieutenant Jackson, near Pukekohe, five miles from Drury, and two miles west of the Great South Road; the natives were repulsed with loss, and a Ranger was wounded. The natives also fired on the 65th's post at Razorback Hill.

On the 9th September, Captain Greaves
guided a party of the 40th Regiment, under
Major Blyth, from the Queen's Redoubt, through
the bush to Tuakau; and another party of the
65th, under Lieutenant Warren, to search for
missing soldiers of the 65th, of Captain Swift's
party; and near Cameron they found the body
of private Grace, covered with fern, with a
gunshot wound in the face, and a cut from a
tomahawk in the chin. The pah was deserted
and the huts gutted, and the stores and forage
scattered about. One of the missing soldiers
paddled himself up to Tuakau in a canoe.

A party of the 18th Royal Irish, under command of Major Lyon, late 92nd Highlanders,
also Militia Volunteers, Auckland and Waeroa
Rifles, were actively engaged against parties of
Maoris attacking and plundering settlers' houses.

Major Lyon was ably supported by Lieutenant
Rupell, 18th, Lieutenant Jones, Militia Volunteers, Ensign Tole, A.R.V., and Mr. McDonald,
native interpreter, Lieutenant State and Ensign
Johnson, Waeroa Rifles, and Quartermaster-

Sergeant Davies, 3rd Battalion Auckland Militia.

Lieutenant-Colonel Chapman, 18th Royal Irish, commanding at Drury, received a report from a Militia officer, Captain Moir, that his drays conveying stores had broken down at a bad part of the road not far from Pukekohe, and that firing was heard towards the stockade there. Captain Inman in command of a party immediately hastened towards the stockade, and found the enemy surrounding and firing into it; a sharp skirmish of an hour ensued, when the enemy withdrew, firing and shouting, leaving twelve men killed. The loss of the troops was three men killed, and Captain Saltmarshe, 70th, and six men, wounded.

CHAPTER V.

The scene changes to Taranaki—Ambuscades planted by the troops—Skirmishes with the enemy—General Galloway—The Maoris advance to attack Poutoko—Major Butler and Captain Shortt engage the enemy—The wounded nobly assisted —Activity of the officers of the Rangers—A repulse in the province of Auckland of Lieut. Lusk's party—Expedition to the Thames, and its object—General Cameron reconnoitres the enemy's position at Meri-meri—The works there are abandoned and occupied by the troops.

THE scene now changes for a time to Taranaki. Captain Russell, 57th, was in command of the party at Poutoko, and on advising with Mr. Carrington, of the Native department, it was determined to plant an ambuscade and surprise the natives near the post. Accordingly officers and men, to the number of ninety, went out on the 15th of September, and were placed under cover on both sides of the Wairao road. After waiting two hours, eight men of the enemy came on within three yards of the party; they then detected a foot-print, carelessly left by one of the soldiers, and calling out to alarm their main body attempted to escape. On this the men immediately fired, and three natives fell, one apparently a chief of some note, as he carried a very handsome taiaha or carved spear (now in the Royal United Service Institution). The wounded Maoris staggered into the bush, and Captain Russell then skirmished with the main body of the natives, whom he drove back to a swamp; other natives, to the number of two or three hundred, coming down from the high ground, attempted to cut off the party from the redoubt, but the camp was regained without loss. The officers creditably assisting in this affair, were Lieutenant Manners and Ensign Powys, 57th, and Staff Assistant-Surgeon Tomlinson.

Colonel Warre, commanding the troops in the Taranaki district, reported on the 26th of September that the military and civil forces under his command inflicted a severe loss on the enemy.

G

On the 24th of September it was reported that
Mr. Clare, a settler at Bell Block, engaged in
his ordinary pursuits on his own land, had been
fired upon by natives, who were said to be
encamped at a place called Ninia, a short
distance over the boundary. Colonel Warre,
being aware that a number of natives had
lately arrived from the south at Mataitawa, it
was thought probable they might wish to try
their strength against the troops on this com-
paratively open ground. He accordingly directed Major Butler, 57th, to march at 3 A.M. on
the 25th, with a party of 180 officers and men,
on the road toward Mataitawa. Major Butler
placed two-thirds of his men in ambush and
held the others in support in the rear. A party
of natives came along the road, and fire was
opened upon them, and they were followed by
skirmishers as far as the Waiongona river;
the chief Enoka, Wuremu Kingi's brother, fell
on this occasion, and three or four other natives.
Captain Shortt, commanding a portion of the
troops was favourably noticed; he had some diffi-

culty in restraining the impetuosity and eagerness of his men to pursue. The troops returned after a fatiguing march of twenty miles in heavy rain.

Colonel Galloway of the 70th, a very zealous and excellent old officer, being now promoted to Major-General, was applied for by General Cameron to be detained in the colony in command of 3000 men, militia and volunteers, in the province of Auckland. He had had the honour of drilling the Duke of Cambridge when he was a young officer.

On the 20th of October a force under the direction of Colonel Warre, C.B., engaged a large body of natives, who had assembled near Poutoko Redoubt, with the intention of attacking it, and after more than an hour and a half's sharp fighting compelled them to retreat with considerable loss. The action was characterised by the gallantry invariably displayed by the troops, and which resulted in liberating the neighbourhood of New Plymouth from the main body of the enemy, who retreated to their pahs, about fifteen miles further south.

G 2

The Maoris, six or eight hundred strong, had advanced to attack Poutoko where Captain Wright, 70th Regiment, commanded, and large fires in various directions were evidently intended to divert attention from the real point of attack.

Major Butler, 57th, was ordered out to Poutoko with eighteen officers and 300 men to reinforce it. He found the Maoris advancing on it from the right and rear of the redoubt, and as the ground was tolerably open he advanced to meet them with about 100 men of the 57th and 70th Regiments.

Colonel Warre coming up, directed Captain Shortt to proceed towards Allan's Hill, and Captains Atkinson and Webster, of the Taranaki Rifles (most useful officers of Bushrangers), to continue the march towards Waireka gully.

Major Butler became engaged with a very superior number of the enemy, who had possession of the bush flanking the fields over which he had advanced. Ensign Powys, who commanded the advance guard, and four men, were wounded ; the enemy's fire was returned, and the men were kept under cover as much as possible, but being greatly outnumbered, they were directed to return steadily to the redoubt.

Captain Shortt now coming up, and attacking on the enemy's right flank, enabled Major Butler to recover his ground, and obliged the enemy to take refuge in the densely-wooded gullies, and from the high trees on the opposite banks they kept up an incessant fire.

Captain Shortt found himself opposed by a very large number of Maoris, who for a time disputed his passage across a narrow neck of land between two gullies, but with determined gallantry his party forced their way across the broken, half-cleared ground, and the arrival of the Volunteer Rifles, under Captains Atkinson and Webster, enabled the troops to become the assailants, and the Maoris were driven into the bush-covered gullies.

During the action, which lasted upwards of an hour, word was brought to Colonel Warre that two or three hundred Maoris had crossed

the Tupae river, and were advancing towards
the redoubt, and firing from Evangi's pah ; a
shell from the howitzer in the redoubt dislodged
them, and a subdivision under Lieutenant Mills
prevented the enemy getting round the flank
between the redoubt and the sea.

The Maoris, finding they could make no
impression, gave vent to their rage by repeated
volleys and frightful yells, after which they
retired.   The troops bivouacked on the ground
in the afternoon, and then returned to New
Plymouth, leaving a reinforcement of fifty men
in the redoubt.

Besides Major Butler, who perseveringly
strove to keep back the enemy, Lieutenant
C. M. Clarke, Deputy Assistant Quartermaster-
General, and Lieutenant Brutton, Garrison Ad-
jutant, ably assisted Colonel Warre, as did also
Acting Adjutant Thompson, 57th Regiment,
Surgeon McKinnon, Captains Shortt, 57th,
and Wright, 70th, Captains Atkinson and
Webster, and Ensign Douglass. Especial notice
of the General was requested to be directed to

the noble conduct of Ensign Down, 57th Regiment, and Drummer Dudley Stackpoole, who, while under heavy fire from natives not forty yards from them, brought away wounded men at the risk of their own lives, their efforts being ably seconded by Private Antonio Rodrigues, a mounted orderly of the Taranaki Militia, who carried two men off the field on his horse, and galloped through a party of natives to take orders to Captain Shortt. Captain Mace and the mounted orderlies generally were of good service in helping the wounded and distributing the ammunition.

The casualties in the action at Poutoko were one man killed and an officer (Ensign Powys) and seven men severely wounded.

In all weather and at all hours Captain Atkinson (the senior officer in command of the volunteers organised to patrol the Taranaki settlement) sought the enemy with his companies, and assisted by Captain Webster and the officers and men under their command, by constantly patrolling New Plymouth and the outskirts of the settlement, kept the enemy in check, laying ambuscades and surprises, co-operating with the regular forces, and cheerfully endured fatigue in the performance of their important duties.

On the 23rd of October an unfortunate occurrence took place not far from Drury. Lieutenant Lusk, in command of the Mauku stockade, hearing that a party of the enemy were shooting cattle at Wheeler's farm at Ti-ti, started from his post with three officers and sixty men, Waikato militia, and Mauku volunteers. The advance party, under Lieutenant Percival, got close up to the enemy under cover of the bush; when discovered, they were hotly pressed by the enemy, and retired skirmishing in good order on the main body without loss. Lieutenant Lusk then advanced with Lieutenant Norman and eight men, and drove the enemy through a strip of fallen timber on to open ground beyond; the enemy then wheeled round on the left flank of Lieutenant Lusk into the standing forest, and being strongly reinforced there, Lieutenant Lusk retired his men. While recrossing the fallen timber the enemy charged from the bush on the left, and after ten minutes' heavy firing within short range, both parties suffering severely, Lieutenant Lusk's party being now outflanked on both sides, he retired his men into the forest on the right, the Maoris not venturing to follow them. The men were then re-formed, and retired leisurely on the stockade.

The casualties were Lieutenants Percival and Norman, and five men killed, one man severely wounded, and one man missing. The officers fell fighting in front of their men. Sergeant Hill and Private Wheeler particularly distinguished themselves by their gallantry. The Maoris' loss was supposed to be sixteen killed, and a great number wounded.

Upon hearing the above, General Cameron immediately ordered Colonel Chapman, commanding at Drury, to despatch reinforcements under Lieutenant-Colonel Nixon, commanding Colonial Defence Force, and Major Ryan, 70th, to intercept and attack the enemy, but he had decamped from the neighbourhood. Colonel

Chapman had previously despatched a party of one officer and eighty men to assist Lieutenant Lusk, but he had incautiously engaged the enemy previously.

From this it will be noted that " sharp practice " was going on in the district of the Great South Road, and that all required to have "their loins girt and shoes on their feet," besides arms in their hands.

The 43rd Light Infantry, and 50th Regiment, and 68th Light Infantry were now ordered to New Zealand from the East, as it was evident reinforcements were urgently necessary.

In November a force of 800 men, regulars and militia, and fifty colonial cavalry, embarked at Auckland under the command of Colonel Carey, 18th Royal Irish, on board H.M.SS. " Miranda " and "Esk," and the colonial steamer " Korio," with instructions to land at Hauraki, on the coast of the Firth of the Thames, and to march from thence to Pukorokororo, a native settlement on the same coast. General Cameron had received information that many of the marauding parties in the bush came from the Thames district, and that Pukorokororo was the point where they landed, and from whence they obtained supplies and reinforcements. Colonel Carey was therefore directed to take possession of the place, and seize all the canoes and provisions he could find, and establish a post there.

It was also intended to establish a line of posts between the Thames and the Waikato to shut out the natives, if possible, from the Auckland district, and reduce the number of posts there, and free the troops in them for operations in advance.

The disembarkation of the troops and horses was very efficiently effected by the Royal Navy under Captains Jenkins and Hamilton without loss or accident. Blue and red jackets worked most zealously together. The natives cleared out, leaving the fires burning in the wharres, with all the furniture, cooking utensils, &c. The Thames has since become famous as a rich gold region.

The steamer " Pioneer " having arrived at

Whangamarino from Sydney, also gun-boats, the " Pioneer " was cleared of stores, and landed two 40-pounder Armstrong guns, which were placed in position to command the landing-place at Meri-meri. These guns were lent to the colony by the Sydney government.

The General proceeded up the Waikato in the " Pioneer," under command of Commodore Sir William Wiseman, to reconnoitre the enemy's works; they occupied them strongly, and fired several shots at the " Pioneer " from the ship's guns they had in position : one shot, shaped like a weight, went through the side of the vessel and lodged in a beef barrel. The ground there being very strong, a further reconnaissance was made up the river, with a view of selecting some point at which a force could be landed to turn the enemy's position, while his attention was occupied in front by the steamer and gun-boats.

The enemy being reported to be escaping in canoes up the Whangamarino and its branch the Mara-marua, it was evident they were abandoning their position at Meri-meri ; and a party of 250 seamen, under Commander Mayne, R.N., and detachments of the 12th, 14th, 18th, and 70th Regiments, numbering in all 500 men, under Colonel Austen, 14th, occupied Meri-meri, capturing the enemy's batteries, and then threw up a redoubt.

The defensive works were directed by Colonel Mould, C.B., R.E., an officer well skilled in Maori warfare.

CHAPTER VI.

THE Waikato, flowing out of the sacred Taupo
lake, in the region of the active volcano, Tongariro, and the snow-clad Ruapehu, is a noble
river, a fine full stream, on which I had formerly
much enjoyment in paddling in canoes when in
command of the outposts of the Waikato. It
had bush on the right hand two miles beyond
Meri-meri, after this it was mostly open country

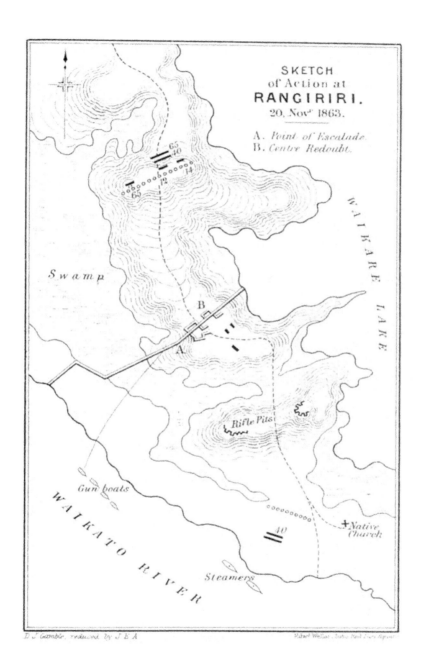

SKETCH
of Action at
RANGIRIRI.
20, Nov.ʳ 1863.

A. Point of Escalade.
B. Centre Redoubt.

WAIKARE LAKE

65
40
2
14
65

Swamp

B

A

Rifle Pits

Gun boats

40

Native Church

Steamers

WAIKATO RIVER

D.J. Gamble, reduced by J.E.A

on either side, the banks occasionally fringed with swamps, but principally bounded by undulating hills. The average width of the river was about 200 or 250 yards, and the current about three miles an hour; 9 feet was the minimum depth of the channel, 18 feet the maximum about Meri-meri.

Rangariri ("angry heavens") was the scene of a very severe action in this war, where many brave men fell, both British and Maoris; the struggle was a hard one—the victory dearly bought. The Maori settlement lay low on the river bank, twelve miles above Meri-meri, and a strong line of entrenchment had been constructed there across the narrow isthmus which divides the Waikato river from the Lake Waikare, thus completely blocking up the road up the right bank of the river.

General Cameron reconnoitred the enemy's position on the 18th of November, in the steamer "Pioneer," and determined on landing a force in rear of the line of entrenchment, for the purpose of cutting off the retreat of the enemy, simultaneously with attacking him in front. He did not care to make a golden bridge for him to escape, and much longer to continue the war.

With this view the head-quarters of the 40th Regiment, 300 strong, under Colonel Leslie, C.B., were embarked on the 20th of November, on board the " Pioneer " and " Avon " steamers, which with four gun-boats proceeded up the Waikato under the command of Commodore Sir William Wiseman, Bart., whilst with a force of 860 officers and men, General Cameron marched from Meri-meri towards Rangariri by the right bank of the river. Both arrived at Rangariri at the same time, 3 P.M.

The troops were halted under the brow of a hill, 600 yards from the enemy's position, and they formed for attack in the following order :— 200 men of the 65th Regiment, under Colonel Wyatt, C.B., on the right, one half in extended order and the rest in support; between these, a detachment of seventy-two men of the 65th Regiment, under Lieut. Toker, with scaling ladders and planks. Captain Brooke, with ten men of the Royal Engineers, was attached to this party.

The detachment of the 12th Regiment under Captain Cole, and the 14th Regiment under Lieut.-Colonel Austen, prolonged the line of skirmishers and supports to the left of the 65th Regiment; Captain Mercer's two Armstrong guns and the naval 6-pounder Armstrong under Lieutenant Alexander, of H.M.S. "Curaçoa," in the centre of the line of skirmishers. The detachment of the 40th Regiment under Captain Cooke and the remainder of the 65th Regiment in reserve.

The enemy's works consisted of a line of high parapet and double ditch, extending, as was before stated, between the Waikato and the Lake Waikare; the centre of this line being strengthened by a square redoubt of very formidable construction, its ditch being 12 feet wide, and the height from the bottom of the ditch to the top of the parapet 18 feet. The strength of this work was not known before the attack, as its profile could not be seen from the river or the ground in front.

Behind the left centre of this main line, and at right angles to it, there was a strong interior line of rifle-pits facing the river, and obstructing the advance of the troops from that direction; about 500 yards behind the front position was a high ridge, the summit of which was fortified by rifle-pits. As the left of the line of the entrenchments could be enfiladed and taken in reverse by the fire from the steamers and gun-boats, General Cameron very judiciously selected that part of the enemy's works for the attack.

The skirmishers of the 65th Regiment were to cover the advance of the ladder party, and, when the latter had succeeded in escalading the entrenchments, were to follow with the support; the whole then bringing the right shoulder forward were to attack the line of rifle-pits facing the river, and having driven the enemy out of it, were to storm the centre redoubt.

The 12th Regiment were to join in the attack on the centre redoubt, and the 14th Regiment to keep the enemy in their front in check until the 65th and 12th Regiments were in the redoubt.

The troops were hardly in position when the enemy opened a heavy fire of musketry from every part of his line, but without effect, the troops being under cover of the brow of the hill.

It had been arranged with Commodore Sir William Wiseman, Bart., that the guns attached to the force with General Cameron and those of the gunboats should, on a preconcerted signal, open fire at the same moment, when the "Pioneer" and "Avon" should also land the 40th Regiment. But the strength of the wind and current rendered the steamers and gunboats almost unmanageable, and at half-past three o'clock, when the signal was given by the General, only one of the gunboats was ready to open fire, and the steamers were still far from the landing-place.

After shelling the enemy's works for an hour and a half, the day being well advanced, and there being little prospect of the remainder of the gunboats getting into position and the steamers reaching the landing-place, the order was given for the assault, the chief influenced by the *perfervidum ingenium Scotorum* and of the old 42nd, in which we had both held commissions.

The whole line of skirmishers and supports rushed eagerly down the slope of the hill, and advanced towards the entrenchment at as rapid a pace as the rugged and uneven nature of the intervening ground would admit, exposed the whole time to a destructive fire from the enemy. Lieut.-Colonel Austen and Captain Phelps, 14th Regiment, and many others were wounded, and fell almost directly on becoming exposed: the enemy's fire was sharp, quick, and heavy, but nothing could check the impetuosity of the assault.

The skirmishers of the 65th Regiment having reached within fifty yards of the entrenchments, and the scaling-ladders having been quickly planted under cover of the fire, the skirmishers and ladder party, followed by the support, mounted the parapet and forced their way over the enemy's first line; then wheeling to the left, and charging up the hill, they carried the second line of rifle-pits, and continued to drive the enemy before them, until their progress was checked by a deadly fire opened upon them from the centre redoubt, which the enemy seemed determined to defend to the last.

The remainder of the troops on the left, finding it impossible to penetrate the enemy's position on that side, joined the attack on the right, and with the 65th Regiment occupied positions round the centre redoubt, almost completely enveloping the enemy.

Soon after the 65th had passed the main line of entrenchment, the General had the satisfaction of seeing the 40th Regiment landing from the " Pioneer " and " Avon," not far from the spot which had been selected. Colonel Leslie, with Irish spirit—without waiting for the companies to form—directed Captain Clarke to take the first fifty men that were landed and attack the ridge in the rear of the enemy's position, whilst he moved with 100 men round its base for the purpose of intercepting the enemy. The ridge, honeycombed with rifle-pits, was carried at once, and a great number of the enemy were killed or drowned in endeavouring to escape across the swamp of Lake Waikare. A portion of the 65th Regiment, after passing the main line of entrenchment, joined the 40th in the attack.

Leaving a detachment to occupy the ridge, Colonel Leslie, with the remainder of his regiment, joined the force engaged at the centre redoubt.

The main line, and some of the inner works, having been taken as described, the troops closed on the enemy towards the centre redoubt, where he now fought with desperation; and the ladders being rather short, he held his ground against every attempt to dislodge him.

The enemy continuing to defend with great tenacity and resolution, General Cameron ordered two successive assaults to be made on the redoubt, the first by the Royal Artillery, armed with swords and revolvers, led by that brave Englishman, Captain Mercer : they were, however, unable to overcome the difficult nature of the work and the heavy fire brought to bear upon them.

Captain Mercer received a severe wound through the jaw and tongue, the shot having been fired through a narrow opening of the enemy's work facing to the rear, which he was crossing in search of a point favourable for making an entry. Every man who attempted to pass that opening afterwards was wounded, except Lieutenant Pickard, R.A. : he received a Victoria Cross afterwards for nobly exposing himself to assist his fallen commanding officer. Captain Mercer, and the other wounded men who fell after passing the opening, could not be moved out till it was masked with earth and planking.

A second assault was made by ninety seamen of the Royal Navy with cutlasses and revolvers, under direction of Commodore Sir William Wiseman and Commander Mayne, of H.M.S. " Eclipse." They went against the front of the work, and were received with a deadly volley, and were also unable to effect an entrance. An attempt was afterwards made by a party of seamen under Commander Phillimore, of H.M.S. " Curaçoa," to dislodge the enemy from his work with hand-grenades, but without success.

It was now dark, and the General resolved to postpone further operations until daylight, ordering the troops to remain during the night in the several positions they had gained.

At daybreak, Colonel Mould, C.B., of the Royal Engineers, suggested that a breach should be made in the redoubt by labour with the pick and shovel, and the operation was in progress when, at six o'clock, the enemy hoisted a white flag, and 183 men surrendered unconditionally, and laid down their arms, though they had a plentiful supply of ammunition. It was understood that the works had been manned at the commencement of the action with 700 men. The surrender of arms is always a trying matter for fighting-men. There was hesitation when the Maoris at Rangiriri were told to give up theirs. At last Te-ori-ori, the chief, handed his rifle to the General, and all then gave up their firearms. Afterwards a leading Waikato chief made a speech : — "We fought you at Koheroa, and fought you well; we fought you at Rangiriri, and fought you well ; and now we are friends, aké, aké, aké " (for ever, for ever, for ever).

The Maoris at once cordially fraternised with our men (I had seen the same occur at Te Arei pah, in the Taranaki), and were particularly good-humoured under their reverse.

Their immediate leader was Te Piori, a remarkably fine-looking Waikato chief, and among the prisoners were several chiefs of note. They were sent to Auckland, and as a temporary arrangement placed on board H.M.S. " Curaçoa."

The list of British casualties amounted to 4 officers killed, 11 wounded; 37 men killed, 80 wounded. Total, 132 killed and wounded.

The loss of the enemy must have been very heavy; 41 bodies were found in and about the works, and a great many were shot or drowned in their flight across the swamp. They must have removed their wounded during the night, as, strange to say, none were found among the prisoners.

The British loss was severe, but not greater than was to be expected in attacking so formidable a position. General Cameron deeply deplored, in common with all under his command, the loss the service had sustained in the death of Captain Mercer, Commanding Royal Artillery in the Colony, who died from the effects of the wound he received while gallantly leading his men to the assault on the redoubt. It was a serious misfortune that the force was deprived of the services of so able and energetic an officer.

Captain Mercer's death was particularly affecting. His wife was sent for to see him in his last moments at the Queen's Redoubt; and as he was unable to speak, from the nature of the wound in his mouth, he wrote with a pencil, " Do not grieve for me. I die contented, and resigned to God's will." This is the true spirit of the Christian soldier.

Colonel Austen's wound was not at first supposed to be mortal, but he succumbed to it. He was an excellent officer, and well liked in the regiment. As an old soldier, I here take the opportunity of giving a warning against the too free use of tobacco. Poor Colonel Austen was a " slave of the pipe," and his system was full of nicotine—hence the wound was difficult to be got over. Mild tobacco, and very little of it (or none at all), is best.*

Captain Phelps, 14th, was a fine young man ; had been educated for a surgeon, and his wound being ·in the groin, he knew well what would be the fatal result, and, like Captain Mercer, he calmly resigned himself to his fate. When the doctor, Assistant-Surgeon Temple,

* The well-known and highly esteemed Bishop Selwyn, of New Zealand, and now Bishop of Lichfield, when visiting one of our camps on the Waikato, said, when I asked his Lordship if I could offer him a cigar, "The Almighty has given me a certain degree of intelligence, and I don't want to obscure it with tobacco." Narcotics are found all over the world for moderate use, not to be abused—tobacco is certainly abused.

R.A., came to dress Captain Phelps' wound, he
said, " Attend to those poor fellows around us;
they may have a better chance than I have, for
I know my wound is mortal;" and the doctor
was obliged to get assistance to compel him to
have his wound dressed.

The General had every reason to be satisfied
with the conduct of the whole of the troops
engaged at Rangiriri.   The 65th Regiment,
under Colonel Wyatt, C.B., and the detachment
of the Royal Engineers, under Captain Brooke,
particularly distinguished themselves by the
impetuosity of their attack on the left of the
enemy's position, and were most gallantly led
by their officers, among whom Captain Gresson
and Lieutenant Talbot (both severely wounded),
with the skirmishers, and Lieutenant Toker,
with the ladder party, were most conspicuous.
Lieutenant and Adjutant Lewis, of the 65th,
collecting a handful of men, gallantly led them
against the redoubt, and was severely wounded
in the attempt.   The rapid and spirited manner
in which the 40th Regiment, under Colonel

Leslie, attacked and carried the ridge in rear of the position reflected great credit on the corps.

The Royal Artillery displayed great daring and intrepidity in the assault on the central redoubt, Sergeant-Major Hamilton, and other non-commissioned officers, standing on the top of the parapet and discharging their revolvers into the work.

Captain Brooke, R.E., was most active throughout the engagement; and after the assault by the Royal Artillery on the redoubt, this officer, with the assistance of Lieutenant Pickard, R.A., succeeded in masking, with planks and earth, the narrow opening in the parapet of the redoubt, through which the enemy had kept up a deadly fire, and prevented the wounded from being removed, among them Captain Mercer. Assistant-Surgeon Temple, R.A., here performed an act of courage and devotion to his duty worthy of record, by passing this opening for the purpose of attending to the wounded, although the extreme

danger of his doing so was pointed out to him;*
every man but one (Lieutenant Pickard) who
had previously attempted to cross having been
killed or wounded.

The advice of Colonel Mould, C.B., R.E.,
and his assistance, were of great value on this
occasion; and the officers of the general staff
did excellent service in carrying out the instructions of General Cameron; as did Lieut.-
Colonel Carey, C.B., Deputy Adjutant-General;
Lieut.-Colonel Gamble, Deputy Quartermaster-
General; Lieut.-Colonel Sir Henry Havelock,
Bart., Deputy Assistant-Quartermaster-General;
Major MacNeil, and Lieutenant St. Hill, Aide-
de-Camps.

Deputy Inspector - General Mouatt, C.B.,
P.M.O., caused the wounded to be promptly
attended to and carefully carried on board the
steamers. The Royal Navy, under Commodore
Sir William Wiseman, gave cordial and most
able support. Prominent in the assault with
their men on the lines and on the redoubt were

* He well earned the Victoria Cross.

Commander Mayne, H.M.S. " Eclipse," and Lieutenant Alexander, H.M.S. " Curaçoa," who were both severely wounded ; as were Lieutenant Downes, H.M.S. " Miranda," and Lieutenant Hotham, H.M.S. " Curaçoa." Lieutenant Murphy and Midshipman Walker, H.M.S. " Curaçoa," were killed.

Captain Lacy, commanding H.M.S. " Himalaya," had marched with the General, and was present during the engagement.

The Maoris had never received such a blow as at Rangariri ; the capture of prisoners and arms they had not been accustomed to (they had always been well prepared for retreat in case of repulse), and what had now occurred they must have regarded as a heavy misfortune. It was hoped at the time it would have had the effect of re-establishing peace on a permanent basis, but this did not occur.

Tents and stores were landed on the 21st of November, the troops encamped in the position, and the construction of a redoubt was commenced.

CHAPTER VII.

NGARUAWAHIA, at the junction of the Waipa
river with the Waikato, was the residence of
the Maori king, and it was desirable that the
Queen's flag should fly there as soon as possible.

The lower Waikato was now open after the
decisive action of Rangiriri—that is, as far as
Taupiri, or fourteen miles above Rangiriri,
where (at Taupiri) the river runs through a

deep gorge, a favourable place for the natives to make another stand, if so inclined.

On the 2nd of December General Cameron moved from Rangiriri, up the right bank of the Waikato, with 850 men, and arrived on the 7th of December at Rahuipokeko, six miles.

On the 8th and 9th the force was conveyed up the river in the " Pioneer," and landed at Ngaruawahia, a distance of about ten miles. No opposition was offered to the advance between Rangiriri and Ngaruawahia, though the latter place was found to be very strongly entrenched.

In ascending the Waikato from Rahuipokeko, the country on either side is flat for a mile and a half ; a gorge is then entered, formed by wooded hills, increasing in height till Taupiri * is reached, when the peak of the conical wooded hill, 800 feet high, rises on the right bank of the river.

Opposite Taupiri was the Reverend Mr. Ashwell's mission station, and at the base of Mount

* Taupiripiri, to clasp round the waist.

I

Taupiri itself was a burying ground of some Maori chiefs, held "tapued," or sacred. Beyond Taupiri the Maungawa flows into the Waikato, and the right bank above the stream continues flat, while the left is closely skirted by a high and beautiful wooded range the whole way to Ngaruawahia, twelve miles. When the troops were advancing up the Waikato in the steamer, to seize Ngaruawahia, a single figure was seen advancing alone to the same point; it was Bishop Selwyn, on the left bank of the Waikato.

The General, after reconnoitring Ngaruawahia in the " Pioneer," and seeing the place was abandoned by the enemy, ordered up a force of 500 men, with camp equipage, from Rahuipokeko. This force, with the head-quarters of the General, disembarked at Ngaruawahia. The British flag was hoisted on the King's flag-staff, and an encampment, with a double line of tents, was formed on a line corresponding with the Delta, between the Waikato and Waipa.

The moral, political, and strategical importance

of the occupation of this place can scarcely be over estimated. Following closely on the enemy's defeat at Rangiriri, associated as the place had been with all the hopes of Maori sovereignty, and standing at the confluence of the great arteries of the Upper Country, its possession became identical in meaning with an important success.

The King's flagstaff, 80 feet high (regularly fitted with cross-trees, &c.), was regarded by the natives as a great type of the "King" movement. From information received it appeared that before the place was evacuated, the Ngatemaniapoto tribe wished to cut this flagstaff down, but the Waikatos resisted. Some shots were fired in demonstration of anger, but the flagstaff was saved by the Waikatos, who said they meant to leave it to the General in evidence of their desire for peace!

Te Wharepu, a high chief of Waikato, who commanded the enemy at Rangiriri, was severely wounded in five places (he was succeeded by Te Piori), and was subsequently removed to the

I 2

head of the Maungatawhiri river. Te Wharepu was visited by Te Wheoro, a friendly chief, and was found to be in a very dangerous state : he sent back to the camp at Ngaruawahia his granddaughter, a fine girl of twelve years of age, as a hostage, and as a proof of his desire of peace. Te Wheoro reported that the Waikatos had expressed their disgust with the Ngatemaniapotos, who, while the former were fighting at Rangiriri, were plundering their houses behind their backs at Paetae and further up. It was difficult to know what to do with the interesting hostage ; she was taken to the General's tent, and got food and a new dress there. Fortunately a relative was found—an uncle—among the friendly natives, and she was consigned to his care.

The progress up the river was necessarily slow, owing to the difficulty of supplying even a small body of troops at a considerable distance from Auckland. There are many shoals in the Waikato, in the New Zealand summer month December, between Rangiriri and Rahuipokeko ; the supplies were conveyed in flat-bottomed row boats. The strength of the current rendered this a most laborious service, but it was performed with great cheerfulness by the officers and men of the Royal Navy, under the personal superintendence of Commodore Sir William Wiseman.

It was understood that the natives had assembled in great force in the front, and had constructed very strong earthworks on all the tracks leading into the interior. In consequence of this, General Cameron proceeded to bring up reinforcements, and collected supplies in order to resume active operations in the field as soon as possible.

On the 28th December the forces moved up the Waipa to Whata Whata, and on January the 1st, 1864, the head-quarters camp was established at Tuhi Karamea, on the Waipa.

The Waipa is eighty yards wide at Ngaruawahia, and towards Whata Whata it narrows to between sixty and seventy, is very winding, and with sluggish stream flows generally between high banks.

The 43rd Light Infantry and the 50th Regiment had now arrived in the colony to co-operate in the Maori war.

General Cameron now thought it desirable to open a communication between Tuhi Karamea and Raglan, a small European settlement on the west coast, having a good harbour, not more than twenty miles distant from the Waipa river, and to which there was only a bush track. He therefore directed the 50th Regiment (the fighting "half hundred") and a detachment of 300 Waikia Militia, the whole under Colonel Waddy (an old Crimean friend), to embark at the Manukau for Raglan, where the greater part had already arrived; more troops were to be employed in improving the track, rendering it *practicable* for infantry and pack horses, so that in case of need reinforcements might reach head-quarters in a few hours, for until this road was made, this line could only be used occasionally for supplies.

Soldiers should be ready at all times to assist with pick and shovel in road making, under the attentive superintendence of their officers. The warlike Romans did as much road making as fighting. It is a pleasure to see trees fall and the bush cleared for a good line of communication; it is a necessary duty, and if there is a good supply of clothes and leather, to meet the unavoidable tear and wear of the service, the duty should be gone about cheerfully, especially as there is working pay usually allowed.

Colonel Warre in the Taranaki had formed a well concerted plan to surprise the enemy's position on the Kaitake ranges near New Plymouth. Lieutenant Clarke, 57th Regiment, Deputy Assistant Quartermaster-General, had volunteered his services to ascertain the line of communication by which the natives had been in the habit of making inroads upon the settlement from the position at Kaitake. Lieutenant Clarke had gone through the bush with one soldier and two natives till he got close to Kaitake, saw it, and returned undiscovered, to report. This led Colonel Warre to attempt a surprise; accordingly he despatched a party of three officers and seventy-two men selected from the 57th and 70th Regiments, Captain Shortt, 57th, Commanding, Lieutenant Clarke and Ensign Pigott accompanying.

It was intended that Captain Shortt's party, guided by Lieutenant Clarke, should arrive at the back of Kaitake at ten o'clock A.M., while Colonel Warre made a demonstration in front to draw the enemy into their rifle-pits from the pah, and leave the ground open for Captain Shortt's party to take possession of the wharres. The parties arrived simultaneously at the time and places appointed; by some mistake Captain Shortt got entangled in the bush, and thought that the enemy had discovered him. The troops in front waiting for Captain Shortt's attack till two P.M., consequently were not allowed to attack, though the regulars and militia volunteers were quite ready to attempt it. A few rounds from the howitzer were fired at the pah. Mr. Parry and some of the mounted men rode within fifty yards of the pah, and were received with a few straggling shots, after which the troops returned to New Plymouth.

As the Duke of Wellington remarked, "If we fail in only one-third of our enterprises we should not complain, but make up our mind to this, as a general rule."

The thanks of the Legislative Council and House of Representatives were conveyed to General Cameron, the Imperial and Colonial forces, for the discipline and valour they had displayed in the late operations in which they had been engaged. General Cameron was also rewarded by the Queen with the Knight Commandership of the Bath, and some of the officers were deservedly promoted.

Captain Greaves, 70th Regiment, Deputy Assistant Quartermaster-General, a very active and intelligent officer, accompanied, from Auckland, on the 16th of November, the Thames Expedition, which was under the command of Colonel Carey of the 18th Royal Irish. The strength of the force was 1000 officers and men and 60 horses. The landing took place without opposition at Hauaratea, on the west coast of the Frith of the Thames. Captain

Greaves was engaged, for several days, with horse and foot patrols, through bush and swamp, reconnoitring the country, and was fired at by parties of the enemy.

After due consideration, three posts were established in commanding positions, to connect the Thames with the Waikato, one was called the " Miranda " redoubt, after H.M.S. of that name, the intermediate was the " Esk " redoubt, and the third the " Surrey " redoubt, after the 70th Regiment; from the position on the Paparata hill (where a strong pah was found deserted and immediately burnt) a commanding view was obtained of the country as far as the Waikare lake, including the Queen's redoubt and the adjacent posts on the west, and a portion of the Thames Frith on the east, and thus signals by telegraph could be established across the country.

A friendly chief, Wiremu Nero (William Naylor), who, with his tribe, the Ngatimahunga, òwned the lands from Raglan on the west coast to the Waipa (had made a road for themselves through the bush towards the Waipa), now waited on the General. The chief, Te Wharepu, died of the wounds he had received at Rangiriri —a brave warrior.

On the 24th of January, 1864, Sir Duncan Cameron marched with a force of 2469 officers and men up the Waipa, from the camps at Tui Karamea and Whata Whata to Te Mamaku, where a halt was made. Colonel Hamley of the 50th Regiment was to march up the left bank of the Waipa to Te Rore, with 444 Infantry.

The steamer, "Avon," came up the river, and Sir William Wiseman landed from it a 6-pounder Armstrong gun and 25 seamen, under Lieutenant Hill, R.N., to co-operate with the land forces. Colonel Leslie, C.B., was detached, with a force of 757 men of the 40th and 65th Regiments, to Ngahiahouri, on the Waipa, to construct a redoubt on each bank of the river. The General marched with the remainder of the force to Te Rore, which he reached on the 28th of January. Thus it will be seen that every precaution was taken by Sir Duncan Cameron to secure the

advance up the Waikato country, and prevent
the supplies being intercepted.

In this manner, in India, his friend Lord Clyde
always acted, and most wisely.

In warfare we should not put out the foot
without being well able to withdraw it again
without "sticking in the mud," or, as our
American friends have it, "First be sure you're
right, then go a-head."

It was easy for some, at a safe distance, to
express impatience at the operations being re-
tarded; the great difficulties of the country were
not understood, and sufficient credit was not
often given to those who did their best to overcome them.

The head-quarter camp was at Te Rore on
the 4th of February. The enemy had not
ventured to oppose the advance of the troops,
although the line of march was crossed at several
points by formidable positions, particularly at
the Manguetama creek, which was passed within
a mile of the enemy's strongest entrenchment at
Pikoinko. For want of sufficient land transport,

the troops marched without tents or baggage. This was really bush-fighting and " roughing."

The troops could only move in single file along the tracks, on account of the high fern on each side ; and bridges had to be constructed across all the creeks, the banks of which were so high and precipitous that roads had to be cut down them to enable the guns and transport carts to pass. Owing to these impediments the troops were a long time on the line of march, although the distance passed over each day was but short.

A depot was formed at Te Rore, preparatory to an advance on Rangiawhia, the principal native settlement in this part of the country. To Rangiawhia, from Ngaruawahia, there were three roads or tracks passable for infantry and artillery. Formidable earthworks had been constructed on two of these, but by the third— the line of the Waipa—it was determined to advance, so as to turn the positions and cut off the enemy's supplies.

The General now hearing that the natives of Turanga, on the east coast, were joining the

Waikatos in great numbers, he proposed to His Excellency the Governor, Sir George Grey, that a force should be sent there to create a diversion in favour of the troops in the Waikato district. A force was accordingly sent there of 652 officers and men, under the command of Colonel Carey, of the 18th Royal Irish; but Sir George Grey did not wish this force to make any aggressive movement without further instructions from him.

The 50th Regiment having been embarked at the Manukau for Raglan, the communication between the Raglan force and the General's field force on the Waipa was established by a difficult path across a high-wooded dividing range, with a mile and a half of bush. At 17 miles from Raglan, 300 Waikato militia garrisoned a redoubt in charge of stores.

In order to relieve the pressure on the supplies of the Waikato, the 70th Regiment was ordered to move from Ngaruawahia to the dividing ridge, and 100 men of the 40th Regiment from Whata Whata to be fed from the

supplies at Raglan. More men were now
urgently wanted for the transport service, and
Colonel Gamble exerted himself earnestly to supply this great want, and obtained volunteers, also
bought additional boats from the ships in Auckland harbour, for the river transport of stores.

The 68th Light Infantry arrived in the colony
from Rangoon.

The 50th and 70th Regiments having crossed
the dividing range between Raglan and the
Waipa, they joined the head-quarters, and put up
their blankets as *tentes d'abris*, after the manner
formerly noticed ; the fern of New Zealand
(as I experienced for months under canvas)
making a most comfortable bed, particularly
if enclosed in some sacking.

Note.—It may be interesting to those fond of Natural History
to notice that the common birds in the Waikato district are
these: the river shag, the grey duck, the wood pigeon of New
Zealand, the parson bird of New Zealand, the bell bird, the
kaka parrot, the green parrakeet, the native robin, and the grey
warbler.

The lizards are the *Naultinus elegans*, a beautiful peagreen
reptile with golden yellow markings, the *N. punctatus*, a tree
lizard with a marbled brown skin, and the common ground
lizard ; though all these are quite harmless, yet the Maoris
seemed to dread them. There are no snakes in New Zealand.

CHAPTER VIII.

Movement on Rangiawhia—A bathing party attacked by the
Maoris—A sharp skirmish ensues—Officers engaged—Captain
Heaphy earns the Victoria Cross—March to turn the flank
of the enemy—Maori sentries—Desperate resistance of the
natives—Colonel Nixon killed—The action at Rangiawhia—
The Maori position—Brilliant dash of the 50th Regiment—
Defeat of the Maoris—The troops are thanked—Devoted
services of the Bishop of New Zealand—The military telegraph—The important results of the late movements.

THE movement on Rangiawhia, which it was
intended to make with the view of turning the
line of the entrenched positions constructed with
great labour by the Maoris, was unavoidably
delayed by an accident which happened to the
" Avon," the only means of transport between
Ngaruawahia and the camp at Te Rore; and it
was doubtful, at one time, if the force would
not be obliged to fall back for supplies till the
damaged " Avon " was repaired. The labour
and trouble attending the getting up supplies

RANGIAWHIA.

A. Maoris attacked
and repulsed by
picquet of 70th Regt.

B. Main position
assaulted and
captured by 50th.
22nd Feby. 1864.
∘∘∘∘∘∘∘ Troops.
••••••••• Maoris.

MANCAHOHOE R.

Swampy flat
covered with thick scrub

TE AWAMUTU

Scale 2 inches to a Mile.

0   ¼   ½   1 Mile

G. R. Greaves.

Published by Longman, Low, Marston, Low & Searle, Crown Buildings, 188 Fleet St. London.

Edwd. Weller, Litho. Red Lion Square.

from Auckland to the front, were immense : the stores had to be shifted twelve or fourteen times between the base of operations, Auckland, and the depôts, on account of changes of land and water transport.

In the meantime, in order to occupy the attention of the natives, and induce them to believe it was intended to attack them at Paterangi, on the ridge about three miles S.E. of Te Rore, a force of 660 men was posted, under Colonel Waddy, C.B., within 1500 yards of the entrenchment. Whilst in this position, several skirmishes took place between Colonel Waddy's force and the garrison of Paterangi, one of which will be hereafter noticed as it reflected great credit on the troops.

In February, the life of a young officer was needlessly sacrificed. Lieutenant Mitchell, R.N., in going down the Waikato in a steamer, observed some Maoris looking at it from a bank in the woods; they were fired at, the fire was returned, and Lieutenant Mitchell, on the bridge of the vessel, fell mortally wounded.

K

On the 11th of February, about 3 P.M., a party of about fifty men of Colonel Waddy's force, it being hot weather, were proceeding to bathe in the Mangapiho river (a branch of the Waipa), covered by a party of twenty men of the 40th Regiment, when they were fired upon by a number of the enemy, who lay concealed in the fern on the opposite side of the river. The covering party returned the fire, upon hearing which Colonel Waddy immediately sent off fifty men to reinforce the party; a very sharp fire was kept up for some time, the enemy falling back. Seeing that a considerable number of the enemy, from their pah at Paterangi, were scattered about the flat, near the river, further reinforcements of soldiers were sent out, till 200 men were engaged.

Lieut.-Colonel Sir Henry Havelock (who came on the ground, and, as senior officer, took the command,) was engaged till half-past seven o'clock skirmishing with the enemy in a running fight, and also when they took post in an old pah called Waiari, overgrown with brush-

wood. The leading men of the 40th, under
Captain Fisher, were supported on the left and
rear by Captain the Hon. F. Le Poer Trench,
of the same regiment. A party under Major
Bowdler of the 40th assisted to hem in the
Maoris. After much hot firing, the troops were
able to dash across the Mangapiho into the old
entrenchment, over a bridge formed by a single
plank. The banks of the river were here forty
or fifty feet high, and densely wooded. There
were also engaged with Captain Fisher, 40th,
Lieutenant Simeon and Ensign King of the
50th, Captain Doran, Lieutenant Leach, and
Ensign Campbell.

A series of hand-to-hand encounters now took
place between the soldiers and the Maoris
crouching in the thick bush. The soldiers displayed, if anything, too fierce an eagerness to
dash at and deal with the lurking enemy wherever visible. This forwardness cost some valuable lives.

Captain Heaphy, of the Auckland Volunteers,
took charge of a party and ably directed it, and

Captain Jackson, with twenty men of the Forest Rangers, was of great assistance. Captain Von Tempski of the same corps relieved the soldiers who had been skirmishing for four hours.

Captain Heaphy, in gallantly assisting a soldier of the 40th, who had fallen wounded into a hollow, became a target for a volley from the Maoris, at short range. His clothes were riddled with balls, and he was wounded in three places. He was recommended for the Victoria Cross, having continued to aid the wounded till the end of the day.

Assistant-Surgeon Stiles was highly commended for attending to the wounded under sharp fire, and seeing them removed early and carefully to camp.

The British casualties were six men killed, an officer (Captain Heaphy) and seven men wounded. The Maoris left twenty-eight dead in the bush, and two wounded prisoners. It was a severe lesson for them.

The continuance of the supplies up the Waipa was now secured by the arrival of the new colonial steamer "Koheroa." A sufficient supply of provisions being accumulated at Te Rore, the General marched, on the night of the 20th of February, to Rangiawhia, leaving Colonel Waddy in his position in front of Paterangi, to protect the depôt at Te Rore, and to be ready to move to any point of the line of communication that might be threatened.

A large convoy of provisions, with two six-pounder Armstrong guns, Royal Artillery, and one naval six-pounder, were to move next day at daybreak, and escorted by the 50th Regiment, under the command of Brevet-Colonel Weare. Tents were struck after dark, and at 11 P.M. the troops paraded, without sound of bugle, and moved silently in the following order :—

Captain Von Tempski, Forest Rangers, advance guard,

Detachment Royal Engineers,
65th Regiment,
70th Regiment,
Detachment of Seamen and Marines,

Royal Artillery Mounted Corps,

Colonial Defence Corps,

Captain Jackson's Company of Forest Rangers
as rear guard.

The success of the movement to outflank and
take the enemy in rear, depended on the secrecy
with which it was conducted. The column had
to pass within 1500 yards of the enemy's works,
and this was done with a noiselessness and
care which reflected the greatest credit on the
discipline of the troops. The enemy's sentries were heard at midnight calling out, as
usual, in evidence of their alertness, as " I see
you, ye dogs! come on and fight; come on!"
meanwhile the column was quietly fording the
Mangapiho and turning his left.

After the passage of the Waipa, the route
lay by an unfrequented track, for four miles,
over a fern ridge, and then came out on a
native dray road, leading from the Punia to Te
Awamutu, a Government school and mission
station, which the natives had compelled the
European residents to leave some months ago.

The buildings were uninjured. The force pushed on at once to Rangiawhia, four miles distant, and the main source of the enemy's supplies.

On approaching this settlement, the cavalry were rapidly thrown forward, and surprised the inhabitants, who were few in number, the greater part of the male population being probably at Paterangi.

The native huts, with walls of raupo or reeds, and thatched with toé-toé grass, were generally scattered over a considerable area, but at one point, where six or seven stood together, a party of armed natives offered a desperate resistance, defending themselves in one of the huts to the last extremity. Here two of the Colonial Defence Force were killed in attempting to effect an entrance, and on the Forest Rangers and the 65th Regiment coming up in support, one of the latter fell mortally wounded. The Maoris pushed their guns through the walls and fired. The door was attempted to be forced open. They pulled a

Ranger inside, and the hut took fire. The door opened, and a big Maori came out in his blanket, and walked up deliberately to the soldiers and gave himself up a prisoner. No others came out, and in the ruins were found the charred remains of six men and the Ranger. Lieut.-Colonel Nixon (whom I knew in the Crimea in the 39th Regiment), commanding the Colonial Defence Force, a most able and gallant officer, here also received a severe wound in the chest, which proved mortal.

The Colonial Defence Force, General Cameron said, under the command of Colonel Nixon, attained a high state of discipline and efficiency, and they displayed the greatest spirit and gallantry on this occasion.

In this conflict twelve of the enemy were killed and twelve taken prisoners.

Not having a sufficient force both for the occupation of Rangiawhia and the protection of Te Awamutu, Sir Duncan Cameron marched back and encamped at the latter place, where the convoy arrived safe in the afternoon.

At six o'clock in the morning of the 22nd February, a report was received from the officer in command of the advanced picquet, that he had observed a large body of the enemy, about two miles in his front, moving from the direction of Paterangi towards Rangiawhia. Sir Duncan Cameron, believing then that the flank march had had the desired effect of causing the enemy to evacuate his fortified position, and that he was now assembling in force at Rangiawhia in defence of its large cultivations, sent to Colonel Waddy to provide fully for the security of the depôt of supplies at Te Rore, and to join the General with the whole of his available force that evening, at Te Awamutu, whence it was proposed to move the next morning to the attack.

At noon, however, of the same day, another report came that the enemy had commenced to entrench himself at Haeirini, on the road between the camp and Rangiawhia, and Sir Duncan Cameron determined to march out at once and dislodge him.

The following force was immediately ordered under arms, and marched towards the enemy's position :

Royal Artillery Mounted Corps	37
Colonial Defence Force	49
Royal Artillery	28
Royal Engineers	11
50th Regiment	506
65th Regiment	223
70th Regiment	296
Forest Rangers	79
Total, officers and men	1229

Whilst this force was advancing, General Cameron received a despatch from Colonel Waddy, that he believed the entrenchments at Paterangi and Pehopiho were evacuated, Captain Saltmarche, 70th Regiment, commanding at the Waiari redoubt, informed Colonel Waddy of this; and Sir H. Havelock, Deputy Assistant-Quartermaster-General, was sent, with 100 men, to ascertain if this was the case. Colonel Waddy also advanced to Paterangi with 120 men, and it was found empty; not a Maori in this strong position, which was immediately occupied with 200 men of the 40th Regiment, under Major Blyth. The works were very strong and intricate, a deep well was found in the place, and a large store of potatoes. Pehopiho pah was also evacuated, a mile and a-half north of Paterangi.

On reaching the advanced picquets of General Cameron's force, the enemy's skirmishers, (thrown forward a mile from Haeirini,) opened fire at 300 yards, behind a hedge, perpendicular to the direction of the Rangiawhia road, which led over undulating ground up to the left centre of the enemy's position. The General then directed Lieutenant-Colonel Mulock, commanding 70th Regiment, to throw out two companies in skirmishing order and to clear the hedge, which they did in the most spirited manner, driving the enemy's skirmishers before them into the main road, along which they were pursued by the cavalry.

The main body of the force then moved along the Rangiawhia road, while the two 6-pounder Armstrong guns, under the command of Brevet Lieut.-Colonel Barstow, came into action on a ridge parallel to and at 500 yards from the position of the enemy, who now opened a rapid and heavy fire along his line.

The native position extended for about 400 yards along the crest of a ridge commanding the road; it was apparently the site of an old pah, the parapet of which afforded him advantageous cover, which he had commenced to improve.

While the two guns and skirmishers were engaged with the enemy, the 50th Regiment, under Colonel Weare, forming the head of the column, were lying down in the road waiting for the order to assault, in which they were to be supported by the 65th and 70th Regiments. The word being given, the 50th, ably led by Colonel Weare, dashed under a heavy fire at the enemy's position, in a manner worthy of the reputation of that distinguished corps.

The enemy's works could only be approached by a narrow road hemmed in on either side by high fern, through which it was impossible for the men to advance in line or in skirmishing order, and necessitated the position being stormed with only a front of four deep, until within a few yards of the trench and rifle-pits. This compelled Colonel Weare to advance the whole regiment in a column of fours at the double, over some 350 or 400 yards under a very severe and concentrated fire from the enemy, most trying to troops in that formation.

Colonel Weare ordered a small storming party of twenty men, under Lieutenant White, 50th regiment, to break cover in the first instance, to endeavour to draw out the first fire of the enemy. This party was almost simultaneously followed by the stormers, consisting of Nos. 1 and 10 companies 50th Regiment, under command of Captain Johnston and Captain Thompson respectively, and these officers entered the enemy's work at the head of their men, at the same time closely followed by the remainder of the regiment.

Colonel Weare stated that the nature of the ground and formation left little for the commanding officer to do but to place the men in the first instance, and leave the officers commanding companies to fight their men ; and he

was proud to say that officers and men nobly
did their duty under very trying circumstances,
and while exposed to a fire that must have
caused a very large increase to the list of
casualties, had it not been for the dense dust
raised by the men doubling, which partly concealed them.

Drs. Davis and Dempster accompanied the
regiment into action, and attended to the
wounded as they fell. Ensign Doveton, 50th
Regiment, fell dangerously wounded with a shot
through his chest by the side of Captain Thompson, whilst gallantly doing his duty. Lieutenant
Pagan, 65th, was severely wounded through the
right leg.

The enemy, seeing the irresistible nature of
the assault, broke and fled before the 50th as
they entered the position. After reforming the
50th Regiment, Sir Duncan Cameron advanced,
expecting that the Maoris would make another
stand on the church hill of Rangiawhia, which
they might have defended with considerable
advantage ; but they made no attempt to do so,

and continued to retreat precipitately towards Mangatautari mountain, leaving their wounded and dead on the field. The Royal Artillery Mounted Corps and the Colonial Defence Force pursued as far as the ground permitted, and sabred some of the enemy.

The loss of the enemy was forty killed and four of their wounded taken prisoners.

The British casualties were two officers severely wounded, and two men killed and eighteen wounded, in this action at Rangiawhia.

The General especially thanked Colonel Weare and the 50th Regiment for the brilliant manner in which they had assaulted the enemy's position; Brevet Lieut.-Colonel Barstow for the precision of the fire of the Armstrong guns, superintended by Lieut.-Colonel Williams, commanding Royal Artillery in New Zealand; and expressed his satisfaction with the conduct of Brevet Lieut.-Colonel Young, 65th, and Lieut.-Colonel Mulock, 70th, Lieutenant Rait, R.A., and Captain Walmesley of the Royal Artillery Mounted Corps and Colonial Defence

Corps. The General was indebted for able assistance to Lieut.-Colonel R. Carey, C.B., Deputy Adjutant-General, and to Lieutenant Johnston, Deputy Assistant-Adjutant-General.

Lieut.-Colonel Gamble, Deputy Quartermaster-General, and Lieutenant-Colonel Sir H. Havelock, 18th, and Captain Greaves, 70th, Deputy Assistant-Quartermaster-General.

With regard to Colonel Gamble, Sir Duncan Cameron wrote to the War Office—" I beg more particularly to recommend this officer for favourable notice, as, to his ability, zeal, and unceasing attention to his important duties, I am chiefly indebted to the success of the operations." Colonel Gamble was then most deservedly rewarded with the order of the Bath.

Captain Baker, 18th, Acting Assistant Military Secretary and Aides-de-camp Major McNeil and Lieutenant St. Hill, 65th, were zealous and active as usual. Deputy Inspector-General Mouatt, C.B., and his assistants on the field, attended promptly to the wounded.

Colonel Waddy in his command had shown, as

he always did, great intelligence and zeal. Very important duties had been fulfilled by the Royal Engineers under Colonel Mould, C.B.; the roads, bridges, and field works, necessary for advancing the force through and occupation of this difficult country, were most skilfully constructed.

Very important services were rendered by Deputy Commissary-General Jones, C.B., and his officers, and they had great difficulties to contend against to keep up the supplies for the troops in a country destitute of resources, and at so great a distance from the base of operations. Assistant Commissaries-General Rolleston and Bailey were especially noticed; Deputy Assistant-Commissary-General Marshall, for activity and energy; and the transport duties were ably conducted by Lieutenant Travers, 70th Regiment.

The Royal Navy gave continued and valuable co-operation, under Commodore Sir William Wiseman, Bart., and Commander Phillimore, H.M.S. " Curaçoa ;" Lieutenant Easther, H.M.S. "Harrier," in charge of the " Avon ;" and

L

Lieutenant Coddington, H.M.S. " Eclipse," in charge of the " Koheroa."

Sir Duncan Cameron, in justice to his own feelings and those of the troops under his command, expressed the deep obligations they were under to the Lord Bishop (Selwyn) of New Zealand, who gained the respect and affection of both officers and men by his benevolent kindness to the sick and wounded, and by his unwearied attention to the spiritual wants of the force, which he almost constantly accompanied in its progress through the country, at great personal risk and inconvenience.

It was well understood also that his Lordship was always most anxiously looking out for an opportunity to aid in making peace; but that result was not yet to occur, without more exciting " actions and incidents."

Formerly when Bishop Selwyn visited our camps, he carried on his saddle his own low tent and poles, and declined the accommodation of a bell tent which I offered him, and he performed his ablutions independently at the nearest brook.

The military telegraph erected by the Quarter-master-General's department was the first in the North Island. It was first laid from Auckland to the Queen's redoubt; afterwards extended as the frontier was pushed forward : it was worked by soldiers, by direction of Colonel Gamble. Strange the Maoris never cut the wires;—the explanation was that they feared, if they touched them, they would reveal their own movements.

On the 27th February the General moved a force under Colonel Waddy, consisting of the 40th and 70th Regiments, and occupied Kihikihi, a fertile settlement, three miles south-east of Te Awamutu; redoubts were also constructed at Kihikihi, Rangiawhia, and Te Awamutu. It was advisable they should be permanently occupied— the two former on account of the immense quantity of food which they contained, and of which, in order to endeavour to bring the war to a close, it was desirable to deprive the enemy —the latter post as very favorably situated for a depot and base of future operations.

The immediate result of the late movements

L 2

had been the abandonment by the enemy of a
series of fortified positions which could not have
been taken without a heavy loss, the possession
by the troops of a large tract of fertile country
between the Waipa and the Upper Waikato
rivers, and the retreat of the enemy into the
interior, with the loss of the cultivation on
which he chiefly depended for his supply.

KAITAKE.

Captured March 25, 1864.

KAITAKE

Upper Pah

Lower Pah

Rifle Pits

Maori Stockade

Rifle Pits

800 yards

Capt.ⁿ Atkinson T.V.R.

Capt.ⁿ Corbett T.M.

Capt.ⁿ M.ᶜ Kellar T.M.

Capt.ⁿ Wright 70ᵗʰ

Capt.ⁿ Lloyd 57ᵗʰ

Det. 57ᵗʰ

Rocket tube

Cohorn

Capt.ⁿ Russell 57ᵗʰ

Capt.ⁿ Mace T.M. Minstrel Corps

24 p. Howitzers

Det. T.M.

Capt.ⁿ Page T.M. under Major Butler, 57ᵗʰ

Capt.ⁿ Schomberg 57ᵗʰ

Armstrong guns Capt.ⁿ Martin R.N.

OAKURA R.

H. J. Warre, reduced by J.E.A.

Published by Sampson Low, Marston, Low & Searle, Crown Buildings, 188 Fleet Str. London.

Edw.ᵈ Weller, Lith.ᵈ Red Lion Square

CHAPTER IX.

A settler, Mr. Paterson, murdered in the Taranaki — Major
Butler sent to reconnoitre the strong position at Kaitake—
And skirmishes with the enemy—Artillery despatched to
the Taranaki—Outposts destroyed — Considerations on the
destruction of crops—Attack on Ahu Ahu—Colonel Warre's
preparations to assault Kaitake—The place is carried—Services of the officers and men acknowledged by Colonel Warre.

IN the Taranaki, a settler, named Paterson, had
been murdered, and Colonel Warre, commanding, having received a report from Captain
Stapp, Adjutant Taranaki Militia, that the
hostile natives had been seen near the spot
where Paterson was killed, sent parties by different routes with the intention of cutting off
their retreat, and also of destroying the native
position of Kaitake, if found feebly defended.

Major Butler, 57th, was sent with a 24-
pounder howitzer and some rockets under Lieu-

tenant Larcom, R.A., and the available men of
the 57th Regiment, to advance against Kaitake,
and ascertain its condition. Major Butler's
party advanced within 800 yards, and opened
fire from the howitzer, Captain Lloyd's company, 57th, being extended on both flanks to
keep down the enemy's fire, which was considerable, from a gully and rifle-pits. The
howitzer was then advanced 150 yards, but
the Maoris appeared in such force, and opened
a heavy cross fire on the party, and being in a
strong entrenched position, and Major Butler's
force being little over 100 men, it was thought
prudent to retire. A man, 57th, was killed,
and Lieutenant Larcom (who refused to go to
the rear) was severely wounded, and five men,
57th, were wounded.

Kaitake had given much trouble, but it fell
at last. Colonel Warre skilfully conducted
four days' operations against this strong position, which resulted in its fall, and with trifling
loss to the troops engaged, the Maoris abandoning the Patua ranges.

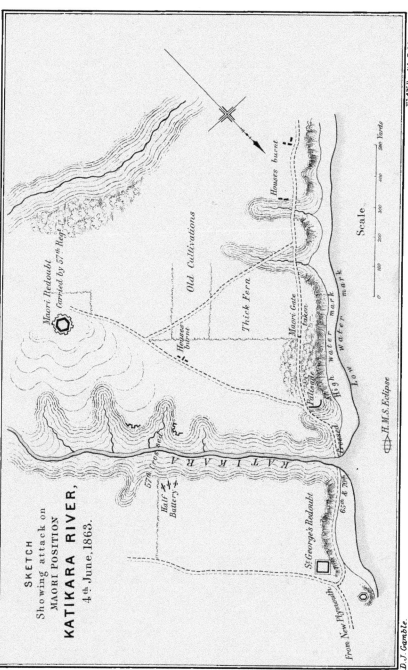

SKETCH
Showing attack on
MAORI POSITION
KATIKARA RIVER,
4th. June, 1863.

Maori Redoubt
Carried by 57th Regt.

Old Cultivations

Houses burnt

Thick Fern

Houses burnt

Maori Gate taken

Palisade

High water mark

Low water mark

H.M.S. Eclipse

Scale.

0   100   200   300   400   500 Yards

KATIKARA

57th. Cross River

Half Battery

65th. & 70th.

St George's Redoubt

From New Plymouth

D. J. Gamble.

Edw.d Weller. litho. Red. Lion. Square.

General Cameron had sent, to aid Colonel Warre's operations, three Armstrong guns and thirty non-commissioned officers and men, under the command of Captain Martin, R.A.

The guns were despatched to Oakura (St. Andrew's redoubt), seven miles south of New Plymouth, and placed in position to try their effect, and shew the natives that they were able to reach their apparently impregnable position of Kaitake on the heights above. The practice was excellent, and it was evident that the fire of the natives could be kept down by the artillery when the troops rushed at the rifle-pits.

Colonel Warre, considering it right to destroy all the out-posts before attacking the main position, left two of the guns at Oakura to keep up an occasional fire at Kaitake, and marched, at 3 A.M. on the 22nd of March, to attack first the Tutu pah. The pah was found to be occupied by only a few women and children, who fled into the bush on the appearance of the troops.

The stockade was pulled down and burnt,

also several wharrés (huts) near it, and some
cultivation was destroyed. This is, unfortunately, the custom of war. I had seen it
done in Africa and in Turkey. I would not
sanction it now, knowing the terrible distress
occasioned to helpless women and children, besides shelter and food gone, and perhaps before
cold and wet. Few things rankle in the breasts
of cultivators more than the loss of their crops,
or render men more savage and *less inclined for
peace,* than fields laid waste ; but it is the custom
of war to do so—" fire and sword " the word.

The chapel at the Tataraimaka block had
been pulled down ; its planking was accordingly
carted off to the Oakura redoubt.

On the 24th of March, another force was
organised to attack the enemy's position at Ahu
Ahu, which crowned the top of a spur of the
ranges, and was higher than Kaitake. The
57th, divided into two parties under Captains
Russell and Schomberg, was supported by
Captains Carthew and Mackellar, of the Taranaki Militia. The two parties meeting at the

top of the ascent, a sharp fire was opened on them by about twenty or thirty Maoris, from a bush-covered hillock on the right of the pah. Two men were wounded, and the horse of Captain Mace of the Taranaki Militia, whilst the soldiers proceeded to cut down the stockade, and make a passage into the interior, when the Maoris made a rapid retreat up a steep and wooded hill in the rear. Great store of Indian corn, tobacco, &c., was found in Ahu Ahu, and a quantity was carted off.

Next day, the 25th of March, it was determined to assault Kaitake. It was arranged that Captain Atkinson, with 150 men of the Taranaki Rifle Volunteers, should gain the enemy's rear by a bush path; that Captain Corbett, with sixty men of the Taranaki Militia, should advance on the left; Captain Schomberg, 57th, and Captain Page, Taranaki Militia, should threaten on the right with 100 men; whilst Captain Russell, 57th, Captains Wright, 70th, and Mackellar, Taranaki Militia, with twenty-five men each, in support of Captain

Lloyd, proceeded up several small spurs on the left, to take in reverse the rifle-pits in front of two pahs which crowned the crest of the hill.

In front of the pahs was a long stockade with rifle-pits behind it, across the upper valley, and the 24-pounder howitzer and a rocket-tube were placed, at 800 yards, in front of this, to endeavour to knock down the stockade. The three Armstrong guns were placed in position on the right bank of the Oakura river, and succeeded in setting fire to a wharré in one of the pahs, and at 10 A.M. the parties simultaneously advanced on the pahs and the long stockade in front of them. Under cover of the smoke of the wharré, Captain Corbett's party immediately rushed at the pah, climbed over the stockade, got into the pah by a zigzag entrance between the two lines of palisading, followed very closely by the assaulting parties under Captain Lloyd, who climbed the spur and rushed at the rifle-pits, from which a heavy fire had been kept up on the centre and right

parties. With a loud cheer for " The Queen,"
the whole pushed rapidly forward.

The party under Captain Schomberg, led by
Major Butler, 57th, mounted the high ground
on the right, and taking the rifle-pits on that
side in reverse, whilst Captain Russell's party,
directed by Colonel Warre, forced their way
through the formidable double line of palisading'
which extended across the valley. The Maoris
escaped from their rifle-pits as speedily as
possible.

Between the high ground on the right and
left, the enemy's line of works extended about
half a mile. The Maoris, concealing themselves
in the fern, for some time kept up an ineffectual
fire, until driven away by rockets and shells
from the Cohorn mortars.

The troops deserved great credit for under-
going so much fatigue as they did, and for their
gallantry during the four days' operations,
ending in the assault and capture of Kaitake
pah.

Major Butler, 57th, was especially noticed for

his cordial co-operation on this and all other occasions; also Lieutenant C. M. Clarke, Deputy Assistant-Quartermaster-General; Lieutenant E. Brutton, Garrison Adjutant; Captain Mace, Taranaki Militia; Staff-Surgeon J. E. Young, and Staff-Assistant-Surgeon M. Jones.

Two taihas, or chiefs' carved spears, were captured at Ahu Ahu, and two Maori flags at Kaitake.

We here give two anecdotes illustrative of Maori character.

During the skirmishing in front of the Paterangi pah, the son of the principal chief fell into the hands of the British; he was badly wounded in the leg. Every effort was made to save the limb, but in vain. Amputation became necessary, after which the patient rapidly recovered. When able to move, the chief was informed that he might send for his son : he did so, and next day a cart-load of potatoes arrived in camp as a present for the General, and a message of thanks for the kind treatment his son had experienced ; the chief also declaring that in future he would not kill wounded soldiers who might fall into his hands, but only cut a leg off and send them back !

After the action of Koheroa, a flag of truce was sent to head-quarters by the Maoris, their object being to obtain information regarding one of their principal chiefs who had fallen, but whose body they had been unable to discover. Major McNeil, A.D.C., with an interpreter, volunteered to meet the Maoris who had been employed all the morning in carrying away their killed and wounded from the scene of action. On reaching the ground, the Major was at once informed that they had found the object of their search. As he wished to ascertain their feelings after their defeat, he asked two or three of the chiefs to share the modest luncheon he had brought with him; and while smoking their pipes, sitting on the hill-side, he conversed with them through the interpreter.

Though depressed from their recent defeat, they seemed confident of being able to prevent the invading force from penetrating into their territory. They declared that they would destroy every soldier who might fall into their hands, giving as a reason that the British had artillery, and they had none. They also said to the Major, " You are now as safe with us as you would be in your own camp; but if we catch you after this, we will not strip you, but we will shoot you, and take your riding boots." On hearing that the General's mess was short of potatoes, they said, " If you will come with us two miles further up the Waikato, we will give you a canoe to return to camp, and will send some baskets of potatoes for the General."

On reaching a creek, several canoes were seen, and the crimson stains on their sides shewed plainly how they had been employed in the morning.

The potatoes were produced, a small but very neatly-made canoe was dragged from beneath some overhanging branches, and Major McNeil and his interpreter, having shaken hands with the hospitable enemy, paddled down the river towards the Queen's redoubt.

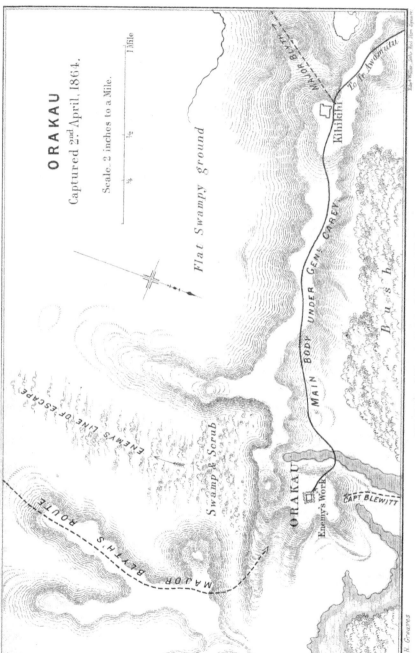

ORAKAU

Captured 2ⁿᵈ April, 1864.

Scale_ 2 inches to a Mile.

1 Mile

Flat Swampy ground

MAJOR BLYTH

To Te Awamutu

Kihikihi

MAIN BODY UNDER GENL CAREY

Bush

ENEMY'S LINE OF ESCAPE

Swamp & Scrub

MAJOR BLYTH'S ROUTE

ORAKAU

Enemy's Work

CAPT BLEWITT

G. K. Greaves.

Published by Sampson Low, Marston, Low & Searle, Grove Buildings, 188 Fleet St. London.

Edwₐ Weller, lithog. Red Lion Square.

CHAPTER X.

ORAKAU. This word will recall to the recollection of troops engaged in New Zealand
warfare a very remarkable or even painful
"action and incident" of the war, 1864, showing
the native character in a new and unexpected
light, and exciting a great desire in the heart
of every true aboriginal protectionist that manly
races should be preserved, improved, and settled
on peace in God's wide earth.

Brigadier-General G. J. Carey's services not being required on the east coast at Tauranga, General Cameron directed him to join the troops in the Waikato, and he commanded at Te Awamutu.

About this time the native orderly, carrying the mail from head-quarters to Pukerimu, was intercepted by a party of the enemy, and neither the native nor the mail was heard of again.

Major McNeil, A.D.C., when returning from Te Awamutu, accompanied by an orderly, was fired on by fifty or sixty natives. His orderly and his horse rolled into a potato-pit concealed in the fern, but the Major did not gallop off, but waited, caught the horse, helped the man to mount, and carried him off in safety to a party engaged in levelling an abandoned pah, and thus secured the Victoria Cross.

On the 30th of March it was reported to the Brigadier by Lieut.-Colonel Haultain of the Waikato Militia, commanding at the Kihikihi redoubt, that natives were seen in force at the village of Orakau, about three miles from his post.

The Brigadier immediately rode over from Te Awamutu to make a reconnaissance, and found the natives were engaged building a pah. It was then too late in the day to attack at once, and he returned to his camp and made arrangements for marching on the enemy's position during the night.

Captain Baker, 18th Regiment, Deputy Assistant-Adjutant-General (a very valuable officer, who had done good service in the Crimea and in India), fortunately found two men in camp, Mr. Gage and Mr. W. Asle, who, from their local knowledge, were at once engaged as guides to enable the Brigadier to determine on a combined attack.

The plan of attack was to advance with the main body along the dray road to Orakau; to detach a force of 250 men under Major Blythe, 40th Regiment, who would take a circuitous route through a somewhat difficult country, crossing and recrossing the Puniu river, and, marching on the right flank of the main body, to take the enemy's position in reverse; and

M

thirdly, to draw a force of 100 men from Rangiawhia and Haeirini, under Captain Blewett, 65th Regiment, who would march across to the enemy's position on the left: the three bodies of troops arriving, if possible, simultaneously before the enemy's stronghold shortly before daylight.

The troops marched as directed; the road from Rangiawhia, by which Captain Blewett had to advance, was found to be difficult, being intersected with deep swamps and thick bush. The Brigadier with the main body, in passing Kihikihi, where Colonel Haultain commanded, took him on with 150 men, and arrived at Orakau as the day dawned.

The enemy, evidently taken by surprise, opened fire on the advance guard, composed of 120 men of the Royal Irish and 20 Forest Rangers, gallantly led by Captain Ring, 18th, and supported by 100 of the 40th Regiment, who immediately rushed forward to attack in skirmishing order.

The position was found to be very strong, on

an eminence, an earthwork with good flank
defences, deep ditches, with a fence of post and
rails outside, and nearly covered from view by
flax bushes, peach trees, and high fern. The
advance guard were forced to retire, but at once
reformed, and being reinforced by another company of the 40th Regiment, again tried to take
the place by assault, but with no better success.
Here Captain Ring, 18th, fell mortally wounded,
Captain Fisher, 40th, severely, besides four men
were killed and several wounded. Captain
Ring had mentioned previously he had a presentiment he was to fall at this place.

On Captain Ring's falling, Captain Baker, 18th
Royal Irish, Deputy Assistant-Adjutant-General,
most gallantly galloped up, dismounted, and
calling for volunteers again endeavoured to enter
the place by assault, and they also failed.

Brigadier Carey finding that there was no
chance of taking the pah in this manner, from
its great strength, and other men having fallen,
he determined to desist from this mode of attack.
Having ascertained that both Major Blythe and

Captain Blewett were at their appointed posts, the Brigadier decided on surrounding the place, and adopting the more slow but sure method of approaching the position by sap, which was shortly after commenced under the able direction of Lieutenant Hurst, 12th Regiment, Assistant Royal Engineer.

At this time Lieutenant Carré, R.A., endeavoured to effect a breach on the enemy's work, but could make no impression on it. A further supply of entrenching tools and some gabions (which had been previously prepared for service on the Horateu or Upper Waikato river) were immediately ordered up with the men's blankets, additional food, &c., and every possible precaution taken, by the proper distributing of the force, to prevent the escape of the enemy.

During the afternoon a reinforcement of some 150 or 200 of the enemy from the direction of Maungatautari appeared in sight, evidently determined on relieving the place. They advanced to a grove situated about 900 yards in rear of the outposts, but seeing that it was scarcely possible to break through the line formed by the troops, they halted and commenced firing volleys, at the same time exciting the men in the pah to increased energy by dancing the war dance and shouting.

Captain Betty, R.A., threw some well-directed shells at the enemy in the bush, which evidently disconcerted them considerably.

The wounded were sent into Te Awamutu and Kihikihi, the sap was pushed forward vigorously, and the troops so posted as to prevent any possibility of escape of the natives during the night. Heavy firing was kept up by the enemy on the troops both in the sap and round the place, during the day and night, causing but few casualties, however, as the men contrived to cover themselves in temporary rifle-pits dug out with their bayonets and hands.

A reinforcement of 200 men, 18th and 70th Regiments, under the command of Captain Inman, joined in the afternoon from head-quarters; and on the proceedings at Orakau being reported to Sir Duncan Cameron, he despatched (and guided

by Captain Greaves, Deputy Assistant-Quartermaster-General) 150 men, 12th Regiment and
Forest Rangers. This party arrived at daylight on the morning of the 1st of April. This
enabled the Brigadier to relieve the men in the
sap more constantly, and to carry on the work
more quickly; Captain Greaves also affording
material assistance in the duties of his department. This day was spent in working at the
sap and making rifle-pits round the pah, few
casualties occurring.

Captain Betty, R.A., being now in command
of the Royal Artillery, enabled Lieutenant Carré
to render some assistance to Lieutenant Hurst
in carrying on the sap, he having been at it
without intermission. During the night a few
of the enemy were perceived trying to effect an
escape from the pah, but being immediately
fired upon, they returned to their earthwork.

At an early hour in the morning of the
2nd April Lieut.-Colonel Sir Henry Havelock,
Bart., Deputy Assistant-Quartermaster-General,
arrived with hand grenades, which were at

once thrown into the enemy's position with great effect by Sergeant McKay, R.A., who there rendered good and gallant service at great personal risk, under a galling fire.

About noon the Brigadier ordered Captain Betty, R.A., to have a 6-pounder Armstrong gun carried into the sap; an entrance having been made, it opened fire on the enemy's works, destroying the palisading, making a considerable breach, and silencing, in a great measure, the fire of the enemy on the men engaged at the head of the sap.

The Commander of the forces, with his staff, &c., arrived on the ground at this time, but allowed the Brigadier to continue his operations without interference with his arrangements.

Colonel Mould, C.B.R.E., coming up with General Cameron, gave his able assistance towards the completion of the sap.

General Cameron being aware that there were many women and children inside the pah, told Mr. Mainwaring the interpreter to call out to the defenders of the pah, " Hear the word of the

General : you have done enough to show you
are brave men ; your case is hopeless ; surrender,
and your lives will be spared." Their reply
was, " This is the word of the Maori ; we will
fight for ever, and ever, and ever ! " (Ka whawhai
tonu, aké, aké, aké!). They were then told,
"Send away the women." They answered,
" The women will fight as well as we ;" and the
firing recommenced.

The Honourable Mr. Fox, late Native Minister
of the colony, in alluding to this, remarked, "Does
ancient or modern history, or our own 'rough
island story,' record anything more heroic ?"

The troops were now getting desperate, a
hand to hand encounter was imminent, and a
private throwing his cap into the ditch jumped
after it. About twenty men, led by Captain
Harford of the Colonial Defence Force, followed ;
the Maoris delivered a withering volley and
ran to the inner works. Captain Harford fell
shot through one eye, and ten men out of the
twenty were down.

Some of the 65th and militia tried the ditch

on the other side, but got no further either. It was now 4 o'clock in the afternoon of the third day's investment and attack on Orakau, during which time all the 300 Maoris had to subsist on was some raw potatoes, and not a drop of water, whilst grape, bullets, and grenades poured into the work.

Suddenly on the south side of the work, invested by a double line of the 40th Regiment, the Maori garrison came out of their entrenchment on to the open, and in a silent and compact body moved on without precipitation. There was something mysterious in their appearance as they advanced towards the cordon of troops without fear, without firing a shot, or a single cry being heard even from the women and children, who with their principal chiefs were in their midst.

As Colonel Gamble observed, "An overwhelming force surrounded them, and all hope of relief had failed, but still, with extraordinary devotion to their cause, calmly in the face of death they abandoned their position without yielding."

The first line of the 40th was disposed under a slight bank, which partly concealed the men from the pah. The Maoris made for this, and it is said jumped over the heads of some of the soldiers, and passing on, walked through the second line.

The cry was now raised, "The Maoris are out of the pah!" the troops quickly rose and started in pursuit of the dark column. The retreating Maoris now quickened their pace, and broke away for a neighbouring swamp and scrub. Here they might have escaped in a body, but were headed by Lieutenant Rait, R.A., and his artillery troopers, and Captain Pye, of the Colonial Defence Corps, and suffered a serious loss in a pursuit of six miles.

It was deeply to be regretted that in the pah and in the pursuit some three or four women were killed, unavoidably, owing to the similarity of dress of both men and women and their hair being cut equally short, rendering it impossible to distinguish one from the other.

The troops were recalled at sundown, and bivouacked around the enemy's late position.

Diligent search was made at an early hour on the 3rd of April for the killed and wounded of the enemy. Their loss was considerable, amounting to 101 killed, besides eighteen or twenty reported by the prisoners as buried in the pah, twenty-six wounded and taken prisoners, and seven taken prisoners.

Besides Captain Ring, 18th, there were sixteen non-commissioned officers and privates killed of the force; and Captain Fisher, 40th, Ensign Chayter, 65th, Captain Harford, Militia, and fifty-two wounded.

General Cameron duly acknowledged the services of Brigadier-General Carey and his officers, among whom were particularly distinguished Captain Baker, 18th, Deputy Assistant-Adjutant-General, Captain Greaves, Deputy Assistant - Quartermaster - General, Lieutenant Hurst, 12th Regiment, A.R.E., Captain The Hon. F. de P. Trench, 40th, A.D.C.

Brigadier-General Carey recommended for

favourable notice, Colonel Leslie, C.B., commanding 40th Regiment, and commanding
detached forces; Major Blythe, 40th; Captain
Blewett, 65th; Captain Vereker, 12th Regiment; Captain Inman, 18th; Captain Cay, 70th;
Captain Betty, R.A., and Lieutenant Rait, R.A.;
Lieut.-Colonel Haultain, commanding Waikato
Militia; Captains Jackson and Von Tempski,
of the Forest Rangers; and Dr. White, 65th
Regiment, senior medical officer in charge of
the field force.

A remarkable instance of Maori determination and endurance may be here recorded.
Captain Greaves, armed with a rifle, had gone
to the head of the sap, and was watching for an
opportunity to enter the pah. He stood behind
the first gabion. Presently the shaggy head of
a very fierce-looking Maori appeared above the
parapet; he was making ready to fire, but
Captain Greaves was too quick for him, and
fired first, and the head disappeared. When
the pah was entered, after the retreat of the
column, Captain Greaves saw a Maori come

forward with a white flag in his hand. A soldier
was rushing at him with his bayonet, when
Colonel Mould, who was by, pushed the soldier
aside, and saved the Maori's life. Captain
Greaves then looked for the warrior he had
fired at. He found him lying dead from a
bullet between the eyes, and one of his legs,
which had been broken previously, was tied up
with flax and a tent peg, to enable him to continue fighting to the last extremity.

Some may remark, on reading this account
of the capture of Orakau, " It would have been
generous to have held one's hand, and not
pursue and fire at the retiring column of
Maoris." Certainly it would; but it is to be
considered that the soldiers had suffered, too,
from the determined resistance of the enemy,
and their blood was up. In a case like this, one
does not pause to reflect, and the dark warriors
had arms in their hands; they might have
turned suddenly and fired into the troops. It
is said that they wounded two or three of the
40th in passing, probably with their toma-

hawks. War hardens the heart, and will do so until a blessed reign of peace prevails on the earth.

A native girl, a great beauty, was found in the pah, severely wounded in the arm, and a corporal proposed to marry her. She was taken every care of, and sent to the Rev. Mr. Ashwell's family, and named Marianne.

Sir Duncan Cameron, whilst deeply regretting that the Maoris did not accept the terms which had been offered, added, in his report to the War Office, " I cannot, in justice, refrain from paying a tribute to the heroic courage and devotion of this band of natives, who, without water and with but little food for more than two days, and deprived of all hope of succour, held out so long against a vastly superior force, and at last, disdaining to surrender, silently and deliberately abandoned their position, under a terrific fire from our troops."

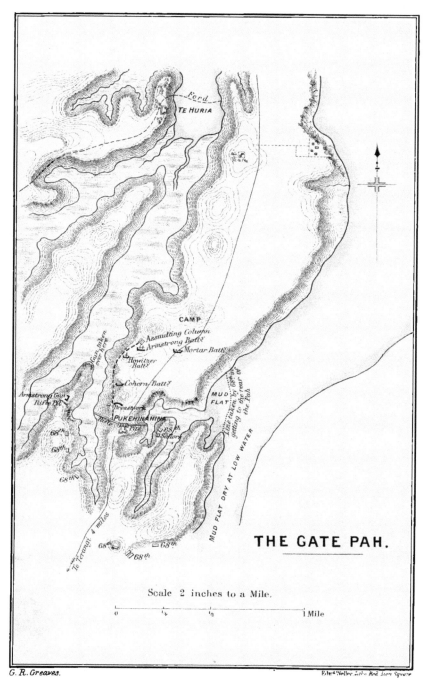

Ford

TE HURIA

CAMP

Assaulting Column
Armstrong Batty
Mortar Batty
Howitzer
Batty
Cohorn Batty

Armstrong Gun
Rifle Pit
Breastwork
PUKEHINAHINA
Rifle Pits
68th
Colours

68th
68th

68th

MUD
FLAT

line taken by 68th of
getting to the rear of
the Pah

68th
68th

MUD FLAT DRY AT LOW WATER

To Tauranga 4 miles

Guns taken over here

THE GATE PAH.

Scale 2 inches to a Mile.

0   1/4   1/2   1 Mile

G. R. Greaves.

Edwd Weller Litho Red Lion Square

Published by Sampson Low, Marston, Low, & Searle, Crown Buildings, 188 Fleet Street, London.

CHAPTER XI.

The Maoris retreat to Mangatautari — Their works there are abandoned—Surrender of a party of natives—Captain Lloyd's party surprised and scattered—Precautions in bush fighting The Gate pah—Preparations for attacking it—Composition of the force—Colonel Greer's night march—68th Regiment posted to intercept the enemy—Feigned attack—Disposal of the troops round the pah—The assaulting column is repulsed—Heavy losses—Particulars of naval officers and men —Maori letters and messages.

GENERAL CAMERON having arranged with his Excellency the Governor, Sir George Grey, that his operations should be directed against Mangatautari, on the Upper Waikato, to which place the Waikatos had retired under the astute leader William Thompson (Wiremu Tamehana). Accordingly, the General reconnoitred the enemy's position closely, and found that it consisted of two strong earthworks, well flanked and palisaded, 450 yards distant from each other, and constructed on a spur of the Puke-

kura* range. The lower work, the largest and
principal one, was 600 yards from the river,
and the two works completely blocked the road
to the settlement of Mangatautari, which was
ffve miles behind them.

Being too strong to be taken by a *coup de
main*, the General intended to try the effect of
vertical fire on the works, and to endeavour to
breach them with howitzers, and caused a
10-inch, and two 8-inch mortars, and two 32-
and two 24-pounder howitzers to be brought up
the river.

A reconnaissance of these pahs at Pukekura
being made by a force up the right bank of the
Waikato, both pahs were found to be abandoned. The 50th Regiment was immediately
ordered to take possession, and encamped on the
ground. The enemy had probably heard of
the preparations in progress for besieging the
place, found their position untenable, and were
in addition, perhaps, pressed for supplies.

Negociations were now going on with the

* Red mountain.

enemy through Wiremu Nero (William Naylor), the friendly chief, and it was agreed to, in writing, by Ruihana, one of the leading men amongst the hostile natives, who had left the Pukekura pahs, that on a particular day 120 men were to come in and lay down their arms. On the appointed day, some ninety women and children, and from twenty to thirty men, came in, and their arms were surrendered; but it would appear that some division took place in their councils, and the rest were deterred from coming in by a rumour spread among them, that if they surrendered they would each have to pay the Government a fine of 10*l.*, besides being put on the roads to work.

His Excellency the Governor arrived at the front on the 16th of April, and next day General Cameron and staff proceeded with the Governor to Auckland, *en route* to Taranaki. The seamen and marines went down the Waikato to join their ships, as it was not likely they would be required in the Waikato country at this time.

N

The 70th Regiment was ordered to march down the left bank of the Waikato to Ngarua-wahia, whence it was to move on to Auckland for embarkation to Taranaki. This reinforcement became necessary in that province, from the following circumstance.

A party of about 100 officers and men of the 57th Regiment and militia went out from New Plymouth on the 6th of April, under Captain Lloyd, 57th, to reconnoitre in the vicinity of Ahu Ahu, near Kaitake. They did not find any trace of natives having been there since the place had been taken; on their way they heard a native shout, but the Maori guide who accompanied the party said he thought it was only a look-out, and that many natives were not in the neighbourhood.

On returning towards their quarters, Captain Lloyd sent Lieutenant Cox, 57th, with a few men to destroy a patch of Indian corn in a gully, leaving the rear guard halted just above on the spur, and halting the remainder of the detachment at the bottom of the spur.

Sufficient precaution was not taken against surprise; and the Maoris, who were on the watch, seeing that the men were scattered after their march, without any guard being posted (and the officers being incautiously separated from their men), suddenly fired a volley from an ambush in the fern, at a distance of sixty or seventy yards, and then rushed at the party with their guns and tomahawks.

Captain Lloyd was wounded, and called to the men to run for the rifle-pits, which were close by. Captain Lloyd shot three natives with his revolver after he fell with a broken thigh, but he was killed with six others, and twelve were wounded. The survivors of the party brought away the wounded, but were not able to save the remains of the slain.

Colonel Warre, on hearing this distressing intelligence, immediately proceeded with a party of regulars and militia, with a howitzer, to discover the Maoris concealed in the bush; and pushing forward, found the mutilated remains of Captain Lloyd and five other men, all of whose heads had been cut off. One of these heads was preserved in the native fashion, by baking with leaves, &c., and carried about with war parties as a trophy, to incite the natives to continue their hostility to the Pakeha. Several men of the militia, who had concealed themselves in the fern, were saved, and brought in by the timely arrival of the party under Colonel Warre. Strict inquiries were made as to the origin of the above unfortunate affair, which served as a caution and a warning in conducting future operations in the bush.

Most old soldiers know that when a reconnoitring party is halted it should be in an open space, or in a defensible position, and sentries should be thrown well out and all round to avoid surprises : if this is done, a vigilant enemy may not attempt a surprise. A fearful catastrophe happened to an army corps at Beaumont, no proper look-out being kept there, during the late Franco-Prussian war.

On one occasion in Caffreland, during the first war there, General Sir Benjamin D'Urban and staff halted in an open space for a meal—a look-out was kept all round.   After the peace, a Caffre said to me, " Do you recollect halting one day at a particular place in the Amatola ? " " Yes, what of it ? "   " I was there in the bush with some others ; we wanted to rush at you, but you were so well guarded we did not venture to do it."

The Gate pah or Pukehinahina—this calls up the memory of a very remarkable and unexpected event in the history of the Maori war.

After the retreat of the Maoris from Manga-tautari, on the Upper Waikato, they dispersed in every direction; and, as it was not considered advisable to follow them any farther into the interior of the country, Sir Duncan Cameron proposed to his Excellency the Governor that further operations should be discontinued in the province of Auckland, that the troops required for the defence and occupation of the territory from which the Maoris had been expelled should hut themselves for the winter (it was now the month of April, the commencement of the Antipodean cold and wet season), and that

the remainder should embark for New Plymouth
to reinforce Colonel Warre, and assist him in
driving the hostile Taranakis and Ngatiruanuis
beyond the boundaries of the settlement.

On the 17th of April, however, information
having been received from Colonel Greer, 68th
Regiment, commanding at Tauranga,* on the
east coast, that the natives in that district had
collected in considerable force, and entrenched
themselves in a strong position at Pukehinahina,
it was decided by the Governor and the General
that the reinforcements intended for New Plymouth should be sent to Tauranga.   They were
accordingly embarked without delay in H.M.S.'s
" Esk " and " Falcon," placed at the General's
disposal for that purpose by Commodore Sir
William Wiseman, and by the 26th of April
the troops were all landed at the mission station
at Tauranga, to which place the General trans-
ferred his head-quarters on the 21st.

On the 27th the General moved the 68th
Regiment, under Colonel Greer, and a mixed

* Landing-place.

detachment of 170 men of the 12th, 14th, and
65th Regiments, under Major Ryan of the 70th,
towards the Maori entrenchment, of which also
a reconnaissance was made. It was found to be
constructed on a neck of land about 500 yards
wide, the slopes of which fell off into a swamp
on either side. On the highest point of this
neck the Maoris had constructed an oblong
redoubt, well palisaded and surrounded by a
strong post and rail fence—a formidable obstacle
to an advancing column, and difficult to destroy
with artillery; the interval between the side
faces of the redoubt and the swamps was
defended by an entrenched line of rifle-pits.

The 68th Regiment and Major Ryan's detachment were encamped about 1200 yards from the
enemy's position on the 27th, and on that and
the following days the guns and mortars intended to breach the position were brought up
to the camp, which was formed by a large force
of seamen and marines, landed at the General's
request from the ships of the squadron by Commodore Sir William Wiseman.

The composition and strength of the force assembled in front of the enemy's position on the morning of the 28th of April was as follows :

General staff, officers	5
Medical staff, officers	3
Naval Brigade, officers and men ..	.. 429
Royal Artillery, officers and men ..	.. 50
Royal Engineers, men	2
Moveable column, officers and men	.. 181
43rd Regiment, officers and men ..	.. 293
68th Regiment, officers and men ..	.. 732
Total	.. 1695

The detail of artillery was as follows :—One 110-pounder Armstrong, two 40-pounder ditto, two 6-pounder ditto, two 24-pounder howitzers, two 8-inch mortars, and six Cohorn mortars.

General Cameron having received information that by moving along the beach of one of the branches of the Tauranga harbour at low water, it was possible for a body of troops to pass outside the swamp on the enemy's right, and gain the rear of his position, Colonel Greer was ordered to make the attempt, with the 68th Regiment; after dark on the evening of the

28th of April; and in order to divert the attention of the enemy from that side, a feigned attack was ordered to be made in his front.

Colonel Greer well executed, with the 68th Light Infantry, the duty assigned to him. At a quarter to 7 P.M. he marched out of camp, each man carrying one day's cooked rations and a great coat. His object was to get in rear of the enemy's position by means of a flank march round his right. To accomplish this it was necessary to cross part of a mud flat at the head of the bay, about three-quarters of a mile long, only passable at low water, and then nearly knee deep, and within musketry range of the shore in possession of the enemy—rough high ground, covered with titri and fern.

At the point at which the 68th got off the mud flat there was a swamp about 100 yards broad, covered with titri about five feet high, on the opposite side of which the end of a spur (which ran down from the high ground in rear of the pah) rose abruptly : this also was covered with titri and fern.

It being of the first importance that the movement should be accomplished without attracting the attention of the enemy, Colonel Greer's instructions were to gain the top of the spur alluded to during the darkness, and remain there till the day showed sufficient light to move on.

The regiment was all across, and lying down in line along the crest of the ridge, with pickets posted round them at 10 o'clock, which was two hours before the moon rose. Colonel Greer acknowledged it was owing to the well-timed feigned attack made by General Cameron in front of the enemy's pah, as was arranged, that the 68th were enabled to accomplish the most difficult part of the march without being attacked at great disadvantage and exposing the movement to the enemy; for when the 68th reached the top of the ridge, the remains of the enemy's picket fires were discovered, the pickets having no doubt returned to assist in the defence of the pah. The feigned attack was made in front by opening a smart fire from the two 6-pounders, assisted by a line of skirmishers.

About half-past 1 o'clock A.M. Colonel Greer advanced his regiment, and at 3 o'clock had reached a position about 1000 yards directly in rear of the pah. He was guided in selecting this position by hearing the Maoris talking in their pah, and by the sentries challenging in the head-quarter camp. It was quite dark and raining at the time.

Colonel Greer now sent Major Shuttleworth forward with three companies to take up a position on the left rear of the pah, and pickets were placed round the remainder of the rear about 700 yards from it. At daybreak Colonel Greer detached three companies to the right, under command of Major Kirby, and posted a chain of sentries, so that no one could come out of the pah without being seen.

Up to this time the enemy did not appear to be aware that they were surrounded, as they could be heard singing and making speeches in the pah. Later in the morning Lieut.-Colonel Gamble, Deputy Quartermaster-General, visited Colonel Greer's post, having an escort

with him of thirty of the Naval Brigade under
Lieutenant Hotham, R.N., and seeing that the
Colonel wanted a reinforcement on his right,
Colonel Gamble left his escort with Colonel
Greer, who was thus afforded valuable assistance.
About this time Major Shuttleworth moved more
to his left and closer to the pah.

These positions were not altered during the
subsequent bombardment, except temporarily,
when the Maoris shewed a disposition to come
out at one or other flank, or when it was necessary to move a little from a position getting
more than its share of shell from the splinters
which kept falling about during the bombardment.

Colonel Gamble returned in safety alone
across the flat to head-quarters.

The guns and mortars being placed in position
in front of the pah, opened fire soon after daybreak on the morning of the 29th of April.
General Cameron gave orders that the fire
should be directed principally against the left
angle of the centre work, which from the nature

of the ground the General considered the most favourable point to assault. The practice was excellent, particularly that of the howitzers, and reflected great credit on the officers in command of batteries.

About twelve o'clock, the swamp on the enemy's left having been reported by Captain Greaves, Deputy Assistant-Quartermaster-General, practicable for the passage of a gun, a six-pounder Armstrong was taken across to the high ground on the opposite side, from which its fire completely enfiladed the left of the enemy's position, which he was thus compelled to abandon.

The fire of the guns, howitzers and mortars was continued with short intermissions for eight hours. The enemy had cleverly planted their flag-staff outside in rear of their oblong work, and the gunners directing their fire at this for a time threw away a good deal of ammunition; but at 4 P.M., when a large portion of the fence and palisading had been destroyed, and a practicable breach being made in the parapet, the assault was ordered.

150 seamen and marines, under Commander Hay, of H.M.S. " Harrier," and an equal number of the 43rd Regiment, under Lieut.-Colonel Booth, formed the assaulting column.

Major Ryan's detachment was extended as close to the works as possible, to keep down the fire from the rifle-pits, with orders to follow the assaulting column into the work. The remainder of the seamen and marines, and men of the 43rd, amounting altogether to 300, followed as a reserve.

When the bombardment ceased, and the signal of a rocket made Colonel Greer aware that the assault was about to take place, he moved up close round the rear of the pah, in such a position that the Maoris could not come out without being met by a strong force. They then made a determined rush for the right rear of the pah, but were met by the three companies of the 68th, and after a skirmish the main body was driven back into the pah ; about twenty got past on the right of the 68th, but they received a flank fire from Lieutenant Cox's party—sixty men of the 68th, and Lieutenant Hotham's thirty men of the Naval Brigade—and sixteen of the Maoris were seen to fall, and a number of men pursued the remainder. The men were collected again, and posted. Lieutenant Trent, 68th, and Lieutenant and Adjutant Covey, gave valuable assistance, also Mr. Parris, who had volunteered as guide.

The assaulting column, four abreast, two soldiers and two sailors, with officers on the flanks, protected by the nature of the ground, gained the breach with little loss, and effected an entrance into the body of the work, excavated and broken up, and with underground defences—most confusing to the assailants, and most advantageous for the garrison. A fierce conflict ensued, in which the natives fought with the greatest desperation with guns and tomahawks.

Lieut.-Colonel Booth and Commander Hay, who led into the work, fell mortally wounded; Captain Hamilton, of the " Esk," was shotdead on the top of the parapet while in the act of encouraging his men to advance. In a few minutes almost every officer of the column was either killed or wounded. Up to this moment the men, so nobly led by their officers, fought gallantly, and appeared to have gained the position; when they gave way, and fell back from the work to cover, under a heavy fire from the parapet. The repulse, without doubt, arose from the confusion occasioned by the intricate nature of the interior, honeycombed with rifle-pits and underground passages; and the enemy lying down had, no doubt, considerable advantage in shooting at our men from concealed positions. The confusion was increased by the men being suddenly deprived of so many of their leaders. This is the natural result in all warfare.

Sir Duncan Cameron coming up, considered it unadvisable to renew the assault at the time. Night was coming on, and he directed a line of entrenchment to be thrown up within 100 yards of the work, so as to be able to maintain his advanced position, intending to resume operations on the following morning, similar to what was intended at the Redan, Sebastopol, in 1855, and the upshot was the same.

The Maoris, taking advantage of the wet and dark night which followed, stole out in small parties from the pah and escaped; several of the posts outside observed them, and fired a volley at them, but could not stop them. The Maoris, careful to expose themselves as little as possible, did not return a shot, except some shots that were fired from the pah to deceive the parties in the rear as to the garrison having left the pah.

On taking possession of the work in the morning, Lieut.-Colonel Booth and some men were found still living, and, to the credit of the natives, had not been maltreated, nor had any of the bodies of the killed been mutilated.

Colonel Booth telling a Maori he wanted water, the young man took a calabash and went outside the pah to the swamp, at great risk to himself, and fetched the water to the sorely wounded Colonel. He had a presentiment he

o

was not to leave Tauranga; and after he got his orders at the General's tent, he shook hands with him, and said, " Good-bye, sir."

It was deeply to be deplored, the loss of so many brave and valuable officers, who fell in the noble discharge of their duty on this occasion. The 43rd Regiment, and the service, sustained a serious loss in the death of Colonel Booth, which took place on the night after the attack. He had set a brilliant example in the assault; and when he was carried out of the work in the morning, and being met by Sir Duncan Cameron, he expressed his regret that he found it impossible to carry out the General's orders.

The heroism and devotion of Captain Hamilton and Commander Hay reflected the highest honour on the Naval Service. Of the 43rd Regiment there were killed, besides Colonel Booth, Captains Glover, Muir, Hamilton, and Utterton, Lieutenants Glover and Langland; of the 43rd, wounded, Ensigns Clarke and M'Coll. Of the Royal Navy, besides Captain

Hamilton and Commander Hay, Lieutenant Hill was killed, and Lieutenants Hammick and Duff were severely wounded. Total, ten officers killed and four wounded; non-commissioned officers and men killed, twenty-one, and seventy-six wounded.

Great regret was felt for the brothers Glover. One could have escaped, but remained to assist his brother; he, too, fell. The younger, still alive in the morning, and suffering, said, "The only satisfaction is Bobby was shot dead."

The losses of the enemy must also have been heavy, although not more than twenty bodies and six wounded were found in or about their position. It was admitted by the prisoners that they carried off a large number of killed and wounded during the night, and they also suffered in attempting to make their escape from the force in rear, which Colonel Greer had conducted on its night march, and had occupied the ground with so much skill. The officers and men of the 68th were accorded the greatest credit for the cheerfulness and zeal with which they performed very harassing duties.

Major Ryan, of the 70th, after covering the advance of the assaulting column with his detachment, followed into the work, and, with Captain Jenkins, of H.M.S. " Miranda," was one of the last to leave it.   Lieutenant and Adjutant Garland, 43rd Regiment, was particularly reported to the General for his conspicuous conduct in the assault.

The commanding officers and heads of departments discharged their duties with zeal and activity; and the services of Deputy Inspector-General Mouatt, C.B., Surgeon McKinnon, 57th Regiment, and Assistant-Surgeon Manley, R.A., who exposed themselves under fire, attending to the wounded, were duly acknowledged.

Commodore Sir William Wiseman, and his seamen and marines, co-operated heartily with the land forces during the operations at the Gate pah.

The enemy having escaped, as described, during the night, at 5 A.M. on the 30th, John Colenutt, A.B. seaman of the " Harrier," entered the pah by himself, and reported that the enemy had left it; and the work was immediately occupied by the troops.

It was with deep sorrow Commodore Sir William Wiseman referred to the casualties among his people, which had been very great, especially among the officers (as at Rangiriri). Captain Hamilton, of the "Esk," was shot through the head while standing on a traverse inside the work, waving his sword and cheering on his men. He was so well known at the Admiralty, and through the service at large, that it was unnecessary to enlarge upon the loss the country sustained in his fall.

Commodore Edward Hay had seen much service in India while serving under the late heroic Sir William Peel, and was badly wounded there. The way in which he led the storming-party into the enemy's work at the Gate pah was the admiration of all; he was mortally wounded by a Maori in a pit below him while cheering his men on, and he died the following day.

Lieutenant Charles Hill, of the "Curaçoa,"

was a most gallant officer; he had been on shore with the men since they first landed, and was killed while advancing and cheering on his men.

Mr. Watt, gunner of the " Miranda," was killed and frightfully tomahawked about the head. Previous to his death he killed with his sword the Maori who shot Captain Hamilton.

The seamen and marines killed were all leading men of the different ships. They, as well as the remainder of the Naval Brigade, behaved with great gallantry. Captain Jenkins, R.N., led the supports up to the work, but they were driven back by the retreating stormers. He succeeded in getting into the pah himself, and was one of the last to leave it.

Lieutenant Duff, of the " Esk," and Sub-Lieutenant Parker, of the " Falcon," were wounded, the former severely, while cheering the men on in the work. Acting Lieutenant Musgrave, of the " Esk," was struck down in the ditch of the work, and for a short time was stunned by a severe blow on the head. He behaved extremely well.

Lieutenant Klintberg, of the Swedish Navy, who had been with the " Curaçoa's " men since they first landed, behaved with much gallantry. Lieutenant Gardiner, of the Royal Marine Artillery, led his men gallantly ; Lieutenant Hammick, of the " Miranda," was wounded severely, close to Sir William Wiseman, while assisting to rally the men retreating from the work ; Lieutenant Hunt, of the " Harrier "— and, indeed, every officer and man—behaved to the Commodore's entire satisfaction.

Among the seamen recommended to the especial notice of the Lords of the Admiralty, Samuel Mitchell was prominent. He was captain of the foretop of the " Harrier." Doing duty as captain's coxswain, he entered the pah with Commander Hay ; and when that officer was wounded, he brought him out, although ordered by Commander Hay to leave him, and to seek his own safety. This seemed to be a fair case for the Victoria Cross.

Richard Smith, boatswain's mate of the " Harrier," highly spoken of by Lieutenant

Hunt of that ship, was one of the first in the work. John Noakes, boatswain's mate of the "Miranda," assisted Mitchell in getting Commander Hay out of the work, and was badly wounded while endeavouring to rally the men, and to prevent their retreating. John Wean, A.B. of the "Esk," was highly spoken of for his good conduct in the assault. James Harris, ordinary seaman of the "Curaçoa," chased a Maori through the work, down the opposite side of the hill, towards the 68th position, and bayoneted him there amidst the cheers of the regiment; unfortunately, in attempting to rejoin his comrades in the pah, he was shot dead close to it.

William Fox, ordinary seaman of the "Curaçoa," who distinguished himself at Rangiriri, was severely wounded in the assault; and gunner William Baker, of the Royal Marine Artillery, carried a wounded seaman out of the pah under heavy fire.

The wounded of the ships were most carefully attended to by Mr. Henry Slade, Surgeon, and

Mr. Robert Harding, Assistant-Surgeon, of the "Miranda," and Dr. Frederick M. Manning, Assistant-Surgeon of the "Esk."

It is a great pleasure to one who has been much associated with the Royal Navy, and made many voyages in ships of war, to offer these records of the sister service which he was allowed to examine at the Admiralty.*

As illustrative of native character, we may mention, that before the force of General Cameron arrived at Tauranga, a native assessor, Patene, wrote to Colonel Greer from Te Papa, the mission station, showing the feeling of animosity in the district that had got head; and on the 28th of March the Colonel got a letter from Henare Wiremu Taratoa, offended at the coming of the troops to that quarter, and adding, " A challenge for a fight between us is declared; the day of fighting, Friday, the 1st of April, is fixed." And this

---

* By an old New Zealand warrior, Admiral Beauchamp Seymour, C.B., and by Sir Alexander Milne, G.C.B., Lords Commissioners.

curious document was also sent to Colonel Greer :—

" *To the Colonel.*—Salutations to you. The end of that. Friend, do you give heed to our laws for regulating the fight. 1. If wounded or captured whole, and the butt of the musket or hilt of the sword be turned to me, he will be saved. 2. If any Pakeha, being a soldier, shall be travelling unarmed, and meet me, he will be captured, and handed over to the directors of the land. 3. The soldier who flees, being carried away by his fears, and goes to the house of his priest with his gun (even though carrying arms), will be saved; I will not go there. 4. The unarmed Pakehas, women and children, will be spared. The end. These are binding laws for Tauranga."

(Signed by five Catholic chiefs.)

In the Gate pah the principal fighting-chief was Rawiri; and when the troops arrived in front of the position, he walked vehemently up and down the parapet, and was heard to say :

" Kia u, kia u, kaore e tae mae te Pakeha "
("Stand fast, stand fast, the Pakehas will not
come hither ").

The manner in which the Maoris defended
their position proved them to be an enemy to be
respected, both for intelligence and courage.
On the first day ground was taken up in front
of them, they hoisted the red flag (on which
was a cross, crescent, and star), and showed
themselves in numbers. Next day no flag
appeared, and no men were for a considerable
time visible. It was only on observing atten-
tively with glasses that one or two heads were
seen to move in the ditch.

During the fire of the guns it was the same,
and it was even thought that the pah was either
deserted or had but few men in it. The readi-
ness with which they stood to their posts and
met the assault, as well as their endurance
during the bombardment, would reflect credit
on disciplined troops.

When the guns opened on them, a voice in
the pah (probably Rawiri) was heard from the

68th side, saying, "Tena, tena e mahi i to mahi" ("Go on, go ahead; carry out your plan"). And again, "Ko te manawarere, ko te manawarere, kia u, kia u!" ("Trembling hearts, trembling hearts, be firm, be unshaken!")

When the assailants retreated from the work, a Maori stood on the parapet and cried, "Pakeha, e ka kapi ahu para pare i o tupapaku" ("Oh, Pakeha, my trenches are blocked with your dead"). It is doubtful, from the distance from which it was heard, whether this was said in triumph or whether it was not said to intimate that the bodies might be removed.

A strong redoubt was afterwards constructed on the site of the Gate pah.

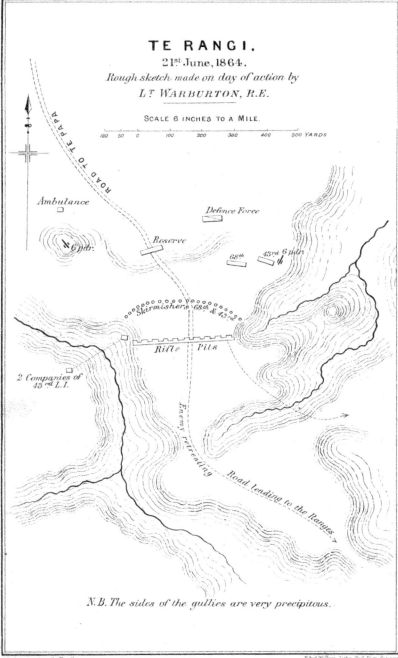

TE RANGI.

21ˢᵗ June, 1864.

Rough sketch made on day of action by

Lᵗ WARBURTON, R.E.

SCALE 6 INCHES TO A MILE.

100 50 0   100   200   300   400   500 YARDS

ROAD TO TE PAPA

Ambulance

Defence Force

6 pdr.

Reserve

68ᵗʰ

43ʳᵈ 6 pdr.

Skirmishers 68ᵗʰ & 43ʳᵈ

Rifle   Pits

2 Companies of
43ʳᵈ L.I.

Enemy retreating

Road leading to the Ranges

N.B. The sides of the gullies are very precipitous.

Reduced by G.R. Greaves.

Edwᵈ Weller, Litho. Red Lion Square.

Published by Sampson Low, Marston, Low & Searle, Crown Buildings, 188 Fleet Strᵗ London.

CHAPTER XII.

Proceedings on the West Coast—Major Butler's flying column—
Deserted pahs burnt — Feuds between tribes on the East
Coast—The post at Maketu—Narrow escape of Major Colville
— The enemy invests the redoubt — Are fired on in their
retreat by ships of war—An Amazon—The troops are hutted
for the winter — The Pai mariri superstition — The priest
Te Ua—Conflict at Motua Island—Extended operations proposed — Remarkable attack on Sentry Hill — Gallantly repulsed by Captain Shortt—Maoris prepare for an attack at
Tauranga—Entrench themselves at Te Rangi — Action and
success there under Colonel Greer—Distinguished services of
individuals engaged—Tribute paid to the troops.

IN April on the West Coast the troops were
not idle, and on the 18th a flying column of
545 officers and men, under Major Butler,
57th, proceeded at midnight from the Oakura
redoubt, southwards, carrying with them four
days' provisions ; 100 men were left at
St. George's redoubt, Tataraimaka, and Major
Butler crossed the Katikara river (where the

action of the 4th of June, 1863, was fought),
and encamped at Wareatea; the deserted pah
of Pukehawa was burnt, some cultivations were
destroyed, and horses of the enemy captured.
On the 20th of April, Major Butler moved a
mile along the coast, and leaving a gun and 150
men in camp, marched his remaining force by a
cross road towards the lower ranges of Mount
Egmont, and found the native pah of Kopua in
a clearing in the bush. Immediately on the
force entering the bush, a rather heavy fire was
opened by the natives, and one of the 57th was
wounded; the fire was replied to and silenced
by an Armstrong gun and the fire of the
troops, but it was not considered necessary to
follow the enemy into the bush, and some
wharrés were burnt, cultivations destroyed, and
more horses captured. The mutilated remains
of Private Gallagher, of Captain Lloyd's unfortunate party, were found on this occasion.

On the East Coast there were two tribes, the
Arawas and the Ngatiporus, who regarded each
other with deadly hatred. The first of these

was friendly to the British. The Government sympathised with the Arawas, and promised them assistance and arms; and Major Drummond Hay, of the Auckland Militia, attached to the Quartermaster-General's Department for interpreting, &c., and Lieut.-Colonel Macdonald, of the Colonial Defence Force (both of whom were excellent Maori linguists), were sent with some of the Forest Rangers to aid and try and discipline the Arawas.

The hostilities between the Ngatiporus and the Arawas became serious, and Major Colville, 43rd Light Infantry, was established at the Maketu pah, south of the Te Papa, and near the coast, to assist the Arawas. The Ngatiporus, about 1000 or 1200 strong, began to construct an entrenched line of rifle-pits, 500 yards long, within 1400 yards of Major Colville's position, Maketu, which was naturally a very strong one, the garrison of which consisted of 160 rank and file, of which 118 belonged to the 43rd Regiment, the remainder to the Waikato Militia.

An engagement took place with the Ngatiporus, two miles from the fort at Maketu, in
which about 110 men of Major Colville's force
were engaged. An ambuscade had been laid
near the ford at Waihi, and when Major
Colville was crossing in a canoe with Ensign
Way, fifty Maoris opened fire on them, and
their escape was wonderful and providential.

Jumping out of the canoe into the water, and
making for the bush, the enemy pursued them
across the ford, yelling and firing. On arriving
at the fort, Major Colville immediately ordered
out fifty men of the 43rd and Waikato Regiment, under Captain Smith, 43rd, to drive the
enemy across the ford. The Maoris recrossed
the river, and established themselves 400 yards
from it, and kept up a constant fire from the
sand-hills and bushes, which was returned with
interest. The enemy mustering strong, thirty
more men were ordered out under Captain
Harris, 43rd Regiment, and Ensign Way of
the Waikato Regiment. Major Drummond Hay
and Captain Macdonald also arrived, with four-

teen men of the Forest Rangers, and a number of the friendly Arawas.

Major Hay was requested to cross the river with his Rangers and all the native allies. This he did, but few of the natives would follow him: after being engaged for some time, he was reluctantly compelled to retire.

Major Colville's orders being stringent not to go far from the Maketu post, he lined the banks of the river, and fired for some time at the enemy at 400 yards. Captain Macdonald, a Royal Engineer, and three of the 43rd were wounded.

On the 26th of April, the enemy advanced his rifle-pits within 800 yards of the post, and continued working at them in spite of the fire of the Armstrong gun; he also sent a message that he intended to attack the post.

The "Falcon" and "Sandfly" men-of-war now appeared, with their black smoke banners, and as there was no shelter from the shells, the Maoris evacuated their trenches, and in a dark column hastened along the beach; hemmed in

P

between the sea and a great swamp, they were helpless under the fire of the ships, and suffered. Another distressing feature in this war, and described in a clever work by Colonel Kirby, 68th Light Infantry, " Henry Ancrum."

Major Hay and his Arawas followed the Ngatiporus as far as Te awa o te a tua, eighteen miles south, and had an engagement there, killing between fifty and sixty, with the loss of one man killed and six wounded (all natives).

This occurred on the 29th, and Major Hay and the Arawas then returned to Maketu.

The leader of the Arawas named Tohi was killed. He had a fine wife, who was much attached to her husband ; she got wild after the engagement, and seizing a musket, shot one of the Ngatiporu prisoners, and thus took revenge or " utu " for the loss of her husband.

It was now the New Zealand winter, and the troops stationed at various posts had commenced to hut themselves in all cases where material was at hand for the construction of temporary shelter. Our Sebastopol underground huts, with a tarpaulin roof resting on the ground, were good, with steps to descend to the interior, and a trench all round for the rain; at other places in New Zealand, where no material was available, huts were erected, and at transport stations, stables of sawn timber.

The health of the troops continued generally good, although there was some fever and dysentery, resulting from the fatigue and exposure of camp life to which the troops had been subjected, many of them for the third season. There was no chance of prize money, as in the East, and they were truly earning "the cheap defence of nations," a military medal.

The "Pai mariri" * faith, as it is sometimes called, or "Hau" superstition, arose and grew during this Maori war. A designing Maori, Te Ua,† seeing that the natives were not successful in their hostility to the British, endeavoured to form a strong combination against them, firstly by superseding the Christian religion (which, under Bishop Selwyn as the leader,

* Good-will.   † The rain.

and other zealous missionaries to the Maoris, had in many places been well established, and was doing immense good), and next by strengthening the movement for the Maori king.

Mr. White, a resident magistrate at Wanganui, said "Pai mariri" began after Kaitake pah was taken by the troops under Colonel Warre, on the 24th of March, 1864, when Captain Lloyd's detachment was surprised, and he and six more men were killed and decapitated, and some of their blood drank, and a head was preserved, as was previously stated.

It was then alleged that the Angel Gabriel, whom the Maoris greatly esteem, appeared to those who had partaken of the blood, and directed the head to be carried through the land, as a trophy and charm against the British bullets.

Te Ua was named as the high priest of the new religion, and assisted by Hapaniah and Rangitauira, these directions were issued : — " The Christian religion is pronounced to be false, and the Scriptures must be burnt, and no

notice is to be taken of the Christian sabbath "
(which used, Scotch-like, to be wonderfully well
kept among the Christian Maoris) ; "marriage to
be abolished. The Angel Gabriel and his legions
would protect those of the Pai mariri faith, and
the Virgin Mary would also be present with
them. The priests would have superhuman
power, and obtain victories by uttering very
forcibly the word 'Hau!'"* (The followers
of this superstition were therefore called
'Hauhaus,' the name pronounced loudly resem-
bling the bark of a dog). "When the head had
completed the circuit of the island, the British
Pakeha would then be exterminated or driven
into the sea."

The prophet Matene, in charge of the head,
first started for the settlement of Wanganui,† and
raised a party of fanatics to attempt to destroy
it; he was opposed by the Wanganui tribe, who
went seventy miles up the River Wanganui to
meet and engage the Hauhaus, challenged them
to a combat on the Island Motua, and a desperate

* A fanatical cry. † The wide river.

conflict ensued.*   At first the Wanganuis were
repulsed, losing about forty men, but rallied,
and drove the Hauhaus off the island, where
forty of their dead bodies lay. The Wanganui
leaders who fell were buried with every honour
at Wanganui, and a monument was raised to
their memory by the Provincial Government.

It was arranged between his Excellency the
Governor and Sir Duncan Cameron that 600
men should occupy the post at Te Papa, at
Tauranga, and 150 men at the Gate pah.   Sir
George Grey also expressed a wish that military
operations should be carried on between Taranaki and Wanganui, to open a road along the
coast.

At New Plymouth many of the Maoris,
deluded by the assertion of the false prophets of
the Pai mariri faith, that they could be rendered invulnerable, advanced on the 30th of
April to attack the small garrison at Sentry Hill,
commanded by Captain Shortt, 57th.   This was

* Well described by the Agent-General in London for New
Zealand, Dr. Featherstone.

a very remarkable affair, and showing the strong delusion under which the Maoris were labouring.

Captain Shortt had observed for two nights a single native coming, by moonlight, apparently to reconnoitre; and then hearing the Maoris in the adjacent bush, he, without the slightest noise or giving evidence of his watchfulness, fell in the men of his detachment at their appointed posts, and made them sit down on the banquette (or step to fire from), with strict orders not to show themselves or to fire until they received the order to do so. The Maoris (reported by the prisoners as over 300 in number) advanced in column to within 300 yards of the redoubt, barking like dogs, and uttering fierce yells, and led by Hapaniah, singing and throwing his arms about wildly. They halted, evidently startled by the unexpected silence in the work, then approached to 150 yards, and some rushed forward.

Captain Shortt called to his men (seventy-five in number) to stand to their arms, and a succession of volleys, with an occasional shell from the small 4½-inch Cohorns by which the redoubt was defended, stopped the Maoris in their advance : they hesitated, broke and fled, leaving thirty-four killed and several wounded, while others were seen to fall, and were dragged off by their comrades.

Major Butler came up with a reinforcement, and pursued the enemy through the bush.

The conduct of Captain Shortt and his Lieutenant, Waller, 57th, was highly to be commended on this occasion, also the strict attention to orders and the steadiness of the men in the redoubt.

The recollection of the unfortunate disaster at Ahu Ahu to Captain Lloyd's party was thus effaced, and confidence was restored. It was ascertained that besides the 300 men who advanced to the attack, 300 more were in support in an adjoining bush, and 200 in reserve at the Mahutahi pah, all ready for an attack on the open ground.

Of the chiefs who fell, Parengi Kingi was the

head, and with him Tupera Keina (Tubal Cain), a large landowner in the Taranaki, Hoerepiriri (Big Joe), &c.

General Cameron having received intelligence from Tauranga that the Maoris were again assembling in force in that neighbourhood, with the avowed intention of attacking the British position, the embarkation of troops at Tauranga was accordingly immediately suspended, and in the absence of General Cameron at the Waikato frontier, Colonel Greer, left in command at Tauranga, on applying to his Excellency the Governor for a reinforcement, he sent him 280 Waikato Militia; Colonel Greer had then 1500 men.

The district occupied by the troops at Tauranga was a peninsula about three and a half miles long, connected with the main land by a very narrow neck, on which was situated the Gate pah, abandoned, as was described, by the natives on the 30th of April, and converted by General Cameron's order into a strong redoubt. This work, and another small redoubt commanding the only ford by which the Maoris could cross over from the main land to the peninsula, rendered the position so secure that when Colonel Greer's report reached the General, he felt sure the Maoris would not venture to attack it. Considering, however, it was not unlikely that they might attempt to construct a pah somewhere in the vicinity of the British position, the General instructed Colonel Greer to watch their movements closely, to patrol frequently, and if they made the attempt to construct a pah, he was to attack them before they had time to establish themselves securely.

In patrolling the country beyond the Gate pah on the 21st of June, at 8 A.M., Colonel Greer came suddenly upon a large body of natives, who had just begun to entrench themselves about four miles beyond the Gate pah. He at once attacked them, and a smart action ensued.

At the commencement of the attack, Colonel Greer had with him about 600 men, and the Maoris mustered about the same number.

They had made a single line of rifle-pits at Te Rangi, on a neck of land and across the road, and in a position exactly similar to that at Pukehinahina (the Gate pah). The ravines at the two flanks were very precipitous.

Having driven in some skirmishers the Maoris had thrown out, Colonel Greer extended the 43rd and a portion of the 68th in their front and on their flanks, as far as practicable, and kept up a sharp fire for about two hours, while he sent back for reinforcements—a gun and 220 men. As soon as they were sufficiently near to support, he sounded the advance, when the 43rd, 68th, and 1st Waikato Militia charged and carried the rifle-pits in the most dashing manner, under heavy fire, but which was for the most part too high. For some time the Maoris fought desperately.

Major Synge commanded the 43rd, and had his horse shot in two places, close to the rifle-pits. Major Colville, 43rd, gallantly led the left of the line of skirmishers into the rifle-pits, being himself one of the first in ; Major Shuttle-

worth, 68th, commanded the supports, consisting
of the 68th, and the 1st Waikato Militia, under
Captain Moore.   The supports were brought up
in the most soldier-like manner, and rushed at the
rifle-pits at the critical moment. Captain Trent,
Acting Field Officer, 68th, fell severely wounded
when leading two companies into the left of the
rifle-pits, and continued cheering on the men till
the pits were taken.

Captain Smith, 43rd, was the first into the
right of the line of rifle-pits ; his gallant conduct
was conspicuous, so much so that he was recommended for the Victoria Cross : he was wounded
severely in two places.   Captain Casement, 68th,
was severely wounded in two places, in front of
his company, while leading into the rifle-
pits.   Captain Berners, 43rd, was also severely
wounded in front of the rifle-pits.   Captain Seymour, 68th, took Captain Trent's place when he
fell, and led his men into the left of the rifle-pits.
Lieutenant Stuart, 68th, was one of the first into
the left line of rifle-pits, and had a personal
conflict with a Maori armed with an Enfield

rifle and bayonet; but Lieutenant Stuart cut him down with his sword.

Captain the Honourable A. Harris, 43rd, was detached to the right in command of two companies, 43rd, to enfilade the enemy's position, and afterwards brought the companies at the critical moment to assist in the assault. Lieutenant and Acting Adjutant Hammick, 43rd, did his duty with great coolness and courage. Lieutenant Grubb, R.A., made excellent practice with the six-pounder at the entrenchment and on the retreating enemy.

Surgeon - Major Best, 68th, P.M.O., and his Assistants, Henry, 43rd; Applin, 68th; and O'Connel, Staff, were most attentive to the wounded. Lieutenant and Adjutant Covey, 68th, and Field-Adjutant and Ensign Palmer, rendered valuable assistance. Lieutenant Covey, when conveying a message to Major Shuttleworth (from Colonel Greer), went with the supports, and was dragged into a rifle-pit by a Maori, who thrust a spear through his clothes. Ensign Palmer was struck in the neck by a musket-ball, and fell insensible from his horse, alongside of Colonel Greer ; when he recovered and had his wound dressed, he performed his duty during the rest of the day.

Sergeant-Major Tudor, 68th, went in front and distinguished himself in several personal conflicts with the enemy in the rifle-pits ; Sergeant - Major Daniels, 43rd, and Acting Sergeant - Major Lilley (70th Regiment) of the 1st Waikato Militia, also distinguished themselves by their coolness and courage ; Sergeant Murray, 68th, whose gallantry and courage were so distinguished, was recommended (with evidence) for the Victoria Cross, and for this reason,—Corporal J. Bryne, V.C., 68th, when the order to charge was given, was the first man of his company into the rifle-pits ; a Maori, whom he transfixed with his bayonet, seized his rifle with one hand, and holding it firm, with the bayonet through him, endeavoured to cut down the Corporal with his tomahawk : his life was saved by Sergeant Murray.

Private Thomas Smith, 68th, severely

wounded, and Private Caffrey, 68th, were distinguished by gallant conduct in the field and prowess in the rifle-pits.

The natives had an intention of attacking Te Papa, but the action at Te Rangi disconcerted them. For an hour previous to the attack, a Maori reinforcement was observed coming towards the rifle-pits, yelling, and firing their guns; and they were only 500 yards from the pits when the advance was sounded.

Besides the six officers wounded, as detailed, there were ten men killed and thirty-three non-commissioned officers and privates wounded. The enemy's loss amounted to 108 bodies buried on the 22nd of June in the rifle-pits dug on the 21st; fifteen wounded, afterwards died; eleven unwounded and twelve wounded prisoners remained in hospital: total, 151 Maoris accounted for.

Both the Light Regiments did credit to their old good name; and it was a matter of special satisfaction that the 43rd had an opportunity, at Te Rangi, of recovering from any depression

they may have felt on account of the unlooked.
for repulse at the Gate pah.

Colonel Greer paid a tribute to the Maoris,
and remarked on their gallant stand at the rifle-
pits; they stood the charge without flinching,
and did not retire until forced out at the point
of the bayonet.

In concluding his report to Sir Duncan Cameron of the action of Te Rangi, Colonel Greer
said, " While in command here (Tauranga), I
have only endeavoured to carry out the instructions given me by the Lieutenant-General commanding; and if I have had any success, it is to
the foresight of these instructions and to the
good discipline and courage of the troops under
my command it is to be attributed."

WAIPARA.

To face page 225.

CHAPTER XIII.

Some native warriors surrender—The forests about Auckland
cleared of the enemy—Discussions about the disposal of the
land—The Governor addresses the Maoris at Tauranga—
An unexpected event occurs—The prisoners sent from the
hulk in Auckland harbour to Kawau island—They break
their parole and escape—They take post on a mountain—
Unsettled state of the south-west coast — Commissariat
arrangements—Successful operations in Taranaki—Te Arei
pah—Mr. Parris— Great meeting of chiefs — A road to be
opened along the south-west coast.

On the 25th of July, 1864, 133 native warriors,
among whom were some chiefs of rank, came
into Colonel Greer's camp at Tauranga, and
laid down their arms. Arrangements were
being made for settling native boundaries by
the Governor, and for confiscating some of the
lands of those who had been most active in the
war.

The effect of the late operations in the pro-

Q

vince of Auckland was that the forests near
Auckland were no longer infested by the enemy;
they were driven about 120 miles beyond them,
and it was understood that, in the middle of
1864, they were suffering severely for want of
supplies of food and clothing, and that their
feeling and intention were not to dispute the
possession of the Waikato, which they considered as lost; and the difficulty in the way
of making peace was the humiliating condition
of giving up their arms, a grievous trial for all
fighting men.

Considerable discussions continued to take
place among the authorities in New Zealand,
civil and military, about fixing boundaries, and
the disposal of the native lands. A meeting
took place at Tauranga between his Excellency
the Governor and the natives there, and it
passed off most satisfactorily. The natives submitted unconditionally to the Queen's authority,
and placed all their lands at the Governor's
disposal. Hostilities were at an end in that part
of the Colony, and there was reason to hope

that the liberal terms accorded to the natives of Tauranga might induce other tribes also to make their submission.

Sir George Grey, in addressing the Tauranga natives who had been in arms, said, " It was right in some measure to mark our sense of the honourable manner you conducted hostilities, neither robbing nor murdering, but respecting the wounded.* I promise you that in the ultimate settlement of your lands, the amount taken shall not exceed one-fourth of the whole land." And to the friendly natives he said, " I thank you warmly for your good conduct under circumstances of great difficulty, and I will consider in what manner you shall be rewarded for your fidelity."

The aspect of affairs in New Zealand at this time appeared to be promising, when an unexpected event occurred, which was likely to disarrange all the plans for the settlement of native affairs in the Colony.

* The watches and money taken at the Gate pah were all given back by the Maoris.

General Cameron had handed over to the Colonial Government about 200 prisoners, who, from time to time, were taken in action against the Queen's troops; these men were to be finally disposed of at the conclusion of hostilities. There being no suitable prison on land for the safe custody of " the wily foe," they were placed in a hulk in Auckland harbour. They were very well treated there, and the Rev. Mr. Baker, of the Church Missionary Society, who gratuitously performed the duty of chaplain to the hulk for several months, stated that the provisions were of good quality and in sufficient quantity, the comfort of the prisoners was promoted in every practicable way, cleanliness and order were enforced, and their moral and spiritual welfare cared for.

A very decided improvement in their appearance was manifested, and expressions of surprise were frequently heard among them of the kind treatment they received at the hands of the Government; the officers in charge were unremitting in their attention to the prisoners, and, in short, under the peculiar circumstances, the Maoris could not have received better treatment.

Ti Ori Ori, the principal chief among them, wrote to his sister, ashore, " Sister ! our place is very good, and also the treatment we receive from our masters."

There was a difference of opinion between Sir George Grey and his Ministers as to the ultimate disposal of the prisoners. The Ministers thought they should be brought to trial as rebels. For my part, I never considered the Maoris as rebels, as they had not acknowledged, that is, few of them, the Queen's authority. They fought so as not to be swallowed up by the white settlers. We went to their country and located ourselves in various parts of it. The old Caledonians could not be called rebels, if they declined to submit to, and fought stoutly against, the invading Romans.

Sir George Grey wished some of the prisoners to be released on parole. His Ministers did not seem to believe in the parole of a Maori, and thought that the imprisonment of these men had a beneficial effect on those still in arms. Sir George Grey had, and has, a beautiful small island, called Kawau, on the east coast, thirty miles from Auckland; and he said if the prisoners were sent there, he would be responsible for them, if landed on their parole that they would not leave the island, which was done on the 2nd of August, from the hulk. His Excellency superintended the arrangements for clearing land and building houses, but there was no military guard there. No suspicion was entertained of an intention, or, seemingly, of the practicability of the prisoners attempting to escape. The island is two miles from the main land, but there were a few boats on the island, and some of the Maoris were observed, before they escaped, to be apparently amusing themselves by making paddles—"aliquando bonus dormitat Homerus" —we are not wide awake at all times.

The persons immediately connected with the charge of the prisoners, were a warden, an interpreter, a medical officer, and the chaplain.

On the night of the 10th of September, silently the Maoris rose, got possession of the boats, and on Sunday morning, the 11th of September, when the bell was ringing for Divine service, and no natives appeared, it was for the first time discovered that they had effected their escape during the previous night, and in doing so must have made several trips with the boats.

It was soon ascertained that after reaching the main land opposite Kawau, they proceeded to the top of a lofty mountain, eighteen miles distant, called Omaha. Mr. White, the interpreter, who had been with them throughout their imprisonment, and exercised considerable influence over them, followed them to their retreat, was received very kindly, and was assured by some that they were sorry for what they had done, and that they determined to return ; they wished, however, they stated, to return with all the rest, who they hoped would accompany them.

A few days more, however, shewed that they

abandoned this idea, if they ever really entertained it, and that they preferred liberty and a
hard life on the mountain, to the restraint and
good treatment they experienced at Kawau.

The escape of these men, at the particular
time at which it took place, was very unfortunate, for there was no knowing to what extent
it might encourage the Waikatos, and the other
tribes to which they belonged, to continue in
arms, in addition to the still greater danger of
the whole of the northern natives, hitherto loyal
to the British authority, being drawn into the
strife. But, happily, no serious disaster resulted
from the escape of the prisoners.

The country between New Plymouth (Taranaki) and Wanganui was the contemplated
scene of the next operations. The natives in
that quarter, who had occasioned the war of
1863 to commence by the cruel massacre of a
party of officers and soldiers, as was described,
had, however, never been met and punished.
But a political difficulty now arose, which occasioned military operations to be deferred. The

Colonial Government was essentially a War Ministry, and having declined to give their assent to the terms offered to the natives in a proclamation which the Governor proposed to publish, they tendered their resignation. Meantime the Governor himself published a proclamation, which allowed the natives, except those implicated in certain murders, till the 10th of December to come in and submit, ceding such territory as might be determined on by his Excellency and the Lieutenant-General commanding.

The General held a considerable body of troops in hand near Auckland, at Otahuhu, in case of any trouble or rising in the north from the presence of the escaped prisoners. All was quiet in the Waikato country.

An admirable report was prepared in October 1864, by Deputy Assistant-Commissary-General Robertson, of the complete and excellent arrangements made by his department for the supply of the troops in a country where all provisions had to be brought from long distances by land and water carriage. This report

was compiled for the War Office at the request
of Commissary-General Jones, C.B.

At the Taranaki a very important object was
attained—the possession of the native positions of
Mataitawa and Te Arei, the latter immediately
overlooking the Waitara, and against which
operations were directed by the sap in the last
war.

Had these places been strongly garrisoned,
their capture could not have been effected without serious loss. But the large body of the
natives there had abandoned them; and Colonel
Warre having received information that the
positions were occupied by a few men, he
accordingly, on the 8th of September, moved
out a force of 500 men, composed of regulars
and militia, and advanced towards Mataitawa,
accompanied by a number of friendly natives.

The direct approach to Mataitawa was blocked
by the entrenchment of Manutahi. The Forest
Rangers, under Major Atkinson, advanced in
skirmishing order to this work, and were received by a fire from the stockade. Major

Ryan, with a company of the 70th, and Captain Martin, R.A., with two guns, came on in support, when the Maoris suddenly abandoned the stockade on its flank being turned.

Manutahi was found to be a strong work, with parapets eight and ten feet thick in rear of the palisading, and casemated covered - ways. The troops pushed on without opposition, and secured Mataitawa, and cut down the flag-staff as a trophy, and destroyed palisading and wharrés.

On the 11th of September, Colonel Warre, with a force of three companies, 70th, under Major Rutherford, and 150 men under Major Saltmarshe, and with an advance guard of fifty friendly natives, marched towards Te Arie pah on its commanding site, overlooking the Waitara, and 300 feet above it; they were assisted by the long sap of last war, which had caused the surrender of the place to the troops under Sir Thomas Pratt. The troops got within a few hundred yards of the pah, and were not discovered for some time, owing to a thick fog

on the river, when a rapid but ineffectual fire
was opened from the pah. It quickly ceased,
and the Maoris, observing a party moving
towards the rear of the pah, abandoned it.

The works were found to be very formidable,

TE ARIE PAH.

ditches fifteen feet deep, and this novelty in
Maori fortification—there was a strong parapet
built of earth mixed with fern, similar to the
system of the Engineers in New Zealand, but

about sixteen feet thick, covered by a line of
rifle-pits or a covered way, about forty yards in
front of the line of the stockade ; so that, had
the guns been used which Colonel Warre took
with him, the Maori defenders, being in front
instead of in rear of the stockade, would have
been entirely under cover. The shot and shell
which would have been naturally thrown into
the stockade, would have been quite ineffectual,
and the garrison would have been able to have
received any attacking column after the palisades
had been apparently breached.

Lieutenant Ferguson, R.E., had the construction of a redoubt on this very beautiful and
commanding position, looking over the wooded
banks of the winding River Waitara, towards
the waters of the Southern Ocean.

In these last operations, and at all times, great
assistance was given by Mr. Parris, assistant
native secretary to Colonel Warre. His knowledge of native character, his practical experience in all matters connected with native
customs, and the great respect with which he

was treated by the friendly natives of both
sexes, enabled him always to obtain reliable and
useful information.

In the beginning of 1865, the natives were in
a very unsettled state all over New Zealand :
great portions of their lands were proposed to
be confiscated (leaving them sufficient, of course,
for their support by industry). The disquietude
was increased by the fanatical belief lately introduced, and spread far and wide, that they
were about to be aided by a special Divine
interposition in driving all the Europeans out
of the island.

A large and important meeting of natives,
hostile and friendly, and which was attended by
the king-maker Wiremu Tamehana (William
Thompson), King Matutaera, Riwi, and other
influential chiefs, was held at Rangitoto, about
twenty-five miles south of Te Awamutu, in
Waikato, for the discussion of the Governor's
last proclamation (regarding confiscation of
land, &c.), and the adoption of final measures
regarding it.

As matters were so unsettled, General
Cameron could not advise or recommend the
withdrawal of troops from the Colony, and
leaving large districts undefended.

Sir George Grey was anxious that a thorough-
fare should be established along the south-west
coast from the Taranaki to Wanganui, that was
closed by the natives, and even the friend of
the Maoris, Bishop Selwyn, was not permitted
to pass along when he tried to do so.

The Weld Ministry of Sir George Grey considered it indispensable to the permanent safety
of Taranaki and to the general pacification of
the country, that a passable road should be
opened along the coast as soon as possible; the
settlements of New Plymouth and Wanganui
should be strengthened and extended; that military posts should be established between the
two; and finally, that as the tribes in the south-
west had always been among the most turbulent
of the native population, had committed the
worst and most unprovoked outrages, and
were then in a state of open hostility, there

could be no permanent peace until they should be reduced to submission and their country opened.

It was there that the dreadful Pai Mariri superstition originated. The natives challenged the troops to fight if road-making went on, and were bold and defiant.

MAORI OUTWORKS.

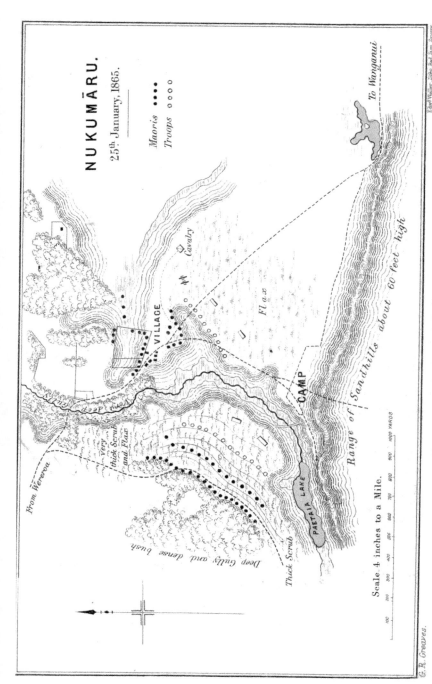

NUKUMĀRU.

25th January, 1865.

Maoris ●●●●
Troops ○○○○

Cavalry

VILLAGE

CAMP

Flax

Range of Sandhills about 60 feet high

To Wanganui

PAETAIA LAKE

Thick Scrub

Deep Gully and dense bush

very thick Scrub and Flax

From Werevoa

Scale 4 inches to a Mile.

100   200   300   400   500   600   700   800   900   1000 YARDS

G. R. Greaves.

Published by Sampson, Low, Marston, Low & Searle, Crown Building, 188 Fleet Str. London.

Edwd Weller, litho. Red Lion Square.

CHAPTER XIV.

Movement to Wanganui—Advance of the troops to the west—
Nukumaru—Pickets attacked—Death of Lieutenant Johnston — Bold attack of the enemy — Charged by cavalry —
Officers conspicuous in the action — General Cameron requires reinforcements — Home authorities wish to reduce
the force—Supplies abundant—Advance on the Patea river
— A smart action with the enemy — His flank turned —
Manutahi — Extensive Maori cultivations utilised by the
troops.

GENERAL CAMERON, in compliance with instructions received from his Excellency the Governor, moved the 50th Regiment and nearly the
whole of the 18th to Wanganui, and intended
also to move his head-quarters there. Colonel
Waddy, C.B., 50th Regiment, was appointed
Brigadier - General. He encamped at Alexander's farm, and on the 24th of January, 1865,
at half-past nine A.M., he marched according to

R

instructions he had received from General Cameron, towards the Waetotara river.

The advance of the troops west was necessarily very slow, owing to the steep ascent of
the road from the beach to the sand-hills of the
Okehu river, and the passage across these hills
of the carts containing baggage and stores.
The force, consisting of Royal Artillery, Royal
Engineers, 18th Regiment, 50th Regiment, and
Military Train (Cavalry), amounted to 963 officers
and men. They reached the kainga or village
of Nukumaru about half-past four P.M. the same
day, where camp was formed close to the Paetaia
lake, and about half a mile from the village.

Immediately after the camp had been formed,
pickets were ordered out, and as a picket of the
18th approached a bush close to the village
which it was necessary to occupy, it was fired
upon by a party of Maoris, who quickly retired
and took up a strong position at the edge of the
bush farther away from the village.

The men of the picket got under cover
behind a railed fence with a small ditch.

Firing was kept up by both sides till dusk, after which it gradually slackened, and ceased altogether about midnight. The Brigadier had to notice, with deep regret, the loss to the service of Lieutenant Johnston, 40th Regiment, Deputy Assistant-Adjutant-General, a most zealous and excellent officer, who proceeded with the picket to see it posted as the Brigadier had directed. He was mortally wounded soon after the firing began, and died next day at noon. Seeing the Maoris were in a strong position, and believing they occupied it in considerable numbers, which might soon be increased from the pah at Wereroa, about three miles off, the Brigadier sent out a reinforcement of 100 men to the front. The Maoris retired during the night, and next morning they were not to be seen or heard in the bush.

General Cameron and Staff joined on the 24th of January. On the 25th, at two P.M., the outlying pickets were suddenly attacked by the Maoris in large numbers, who managed to approach, under cover of the high fern and flax plants, un-

R 2

perceived till close on the sentries. After a short resistance the pickets were overpowered and forced to retire.

Immediately after the firing commenced, all the troops in camp got under arms, and a reinforcement of 100 men was sent to each picket. The attack on the left was soon checked, but on the right the Maoris, setting fire to the flax, under cover of the smoke advanced with great determination, and pushed on through the village of Nukumaru, and got within 150 yards of General Cameron's tent.

The Royal Artillery and Cavalry were rapidly moved to the right, and the guns, six-pounder Armstrongs, were fired into the bush, and drove the enemy out of it. The Cavalry also charged vigorously and effectively over difficult ground.

Nothing like this fight had ever before occurred in New Zealand. Here for the first time a force of 600 natives had appeared in the field, and in broad daylight measured their strength against the Pakehas. Their plan of

attack on both flanks was very good. The
work was commenced with great determination
and spirit, but for want of cohesion failed. The
enemy was beaten by the steady discipline of the
British troops and the excellence of their arms
as compared with the inferior weapons of the
Maoris.

The result of the fight was to raise the Maoris
in the estimation of the troops, and to prove
how readily they learn the European art of war.

They were particularly struck with a charge
of cavalry; and since then large bodies of men
were seen mounted, and cavalry videttes were
observed.

Two wounded Maoris were brought into
camp; one of them a near relative of the chief,
Rewi. The prisoners said that 600 Maoris had
come on to the attack of the position. Twenty-
two bodies were found and buried, and many
more fell and were removed, supposed seventy,
on the 25th of January,—on the 24th the loss
was not ascertained.

The British casualties were heavy, particularly on the left, where the 50th Regiment was engaged, on the 24th of January ; besides Lieutenant Johnston, there were three men killed and six wounded : on the 25th of January there were twelve men killed, and Lieutenant Wilson and Ensign Grant severely wounded, and twenty-four men wounded, many very severely.

Of the officers engaged in these actions, Colonel Weare, 50th Regiment, ably directed a portion of his regiment in the repulse and pursuit of the enemy, as did Brevet-Major Locke, 50th, in command of the first reinforcement. Captain Witchell, Military Train, commanded the cavalry, led his men most gallantly, and kept them well in hand. Major Rocke, 18th Regiment, reinforced the right picket on the 24th, and remained out all night, and was engaged on the 25th of January. Captains Shaw and Dawson, 18th Regiment, did good service with the pickets. Brevet - Major Greaves, 70th Regiment, Deputy Assistant - Quartermaster-General, gave the direction to the cavalry on their advance to the charge, and afterwards was conspicuous in cheering on the infantry when driving the enemy into the bush on the right. Captain Leach, 50th Regiment, the Brigadier's Aide-de-Camp, was of great service in conveying orders.

Brigadier-General Waddy acknowledged the advantage he derived from the presence of Sir Duncan Cameron on the field ; and here, as in the Crimea, the Brigadier's own activity, courage, and good judgment were conspicuous.

Colonel Mould, C.B., Commanding Royal Engineers, was present. Lieutenant-Colonel Williams, R.A., directed the movements of the Armstrong guns. Of the Staff, Colonel Carey, C.B., Deputy Adjutant-General ; Lieut.-Colonel Gamble, C.B., Deputy Quartermaster - General; Major Pitt, Assistant Military Secretary ; and the Aides-de-Camp — Lieut.-Colonel McNeil and Lieut. St. Hill ; were present and ably assisted.

Since the action of Nukumaru on the 25th of January, the Maoris remained quiet in their pah of Wereroa, which stood on very high ground on the left bank of the Waetotara river, about three miles from Nukumaru ; the pah was well fortified and difficult of approach, on account of the dense bush by which it was surrounded. It shall be more particularly noticed hereafter.

Sir George Grey being desirous that five miles of the country, south of the Tataraimaka block in Taranaki should be occupied, this was accordingly done by the troops under Colonel Warre, C.B., as far as the Hangutahua, or Stony river.

General Cameron, considering that two-thirds of his troops were employed in the protection of the different settlements or the occupation of the land taken from the hostile natives, and the natives in his front evidently mustering in force to oppose the advance of the troops, was of opinion that to carry out the views of the Governor and the Colonial Government, a reinforcement of 2000 men would be necessary.

On the night of the 4th of February, Brigadier-General Waddy was directed to march, with a force of 1104 officers and men, from Nukumaru, and to cross the Waetotara, which he did on the morning of the 5th by means of a cask-raft constructed by the Royal Engineers, at a mile and a half from the river's mouth. Colonel Weare, 50th Regiment, was left in charge of the remainder of the troops at Nukumaru.

The head-quarters and 350 men of the 2nd Battalion, 14th Regiment, stationed at Wellington, arrived at Wanganui, and 250 men of the 70th Regiment from Taranaki, to strengthen the force in the south-west.

In February 1865 the home authorities were desirous to reduce the force in New Zealand by five battalions, supposing that the Maoris had been subdued to that extent that such a force could now be spared; yet, from the determined attitude assumed by the Ngatiruanuis in the south-west, they did not seem to consider that they had had enough of fighting, or would yield to the Pakehas.

To save a heavy loss of life by attacking the formidable position of the Wereroa pah, General Cameron resolved to move to the

Patea river, in the hope of drawing the enemy from the pah, and having an opportunity of attacking it hereafter, if necessary, and at less disadvantage.

Accordingly, Brigadier - General Waddy marched with his force, on the night of the 15th of February, to the Patea river; and Colonel Weare, with his detachments, moved from Nukumaru, and took up Brigadier-General Waddy's camp on the Waetotara.

Sir George Grey was desirous of establishing a chain of posts along the coast to the Taranaki; and Sir Duncan Cameron intended to carry out his views as far as the means at his command would admit. In the meantime he was engaged seeing supplies collected at the Patea, and constructing two redoubts on each side of the river to protect them, leaving nothing to chance, and securing his advance. All was quiet at the Waikato frontier, at Tauranga, and at Taranaki, after the operations in this quarter, so well planned and well conducted.

The commissariat supplies were now abundant and excellent, under the direction of Deputy Commissary - General Strickland and his staff. The well-cultivated farms of settlers on the south-west raising wheat and oats, rich clover, abundant well-bred cattle, and Scotch sheep, enabled the commissariat to effect the purchase of ample supplies for man and beast of the force.

H.R.H. the Field-Marshal Commanding-in-Chief, when applied to by the local Government to sanction enlisting from Her Majesty's regiments in New Zealand 1500 men as a colonial defence force, did not approve of that measure, as opposed to Imperial interests.

On the 9th of March, with a view to carry out the instructions of his Excellency the Governor, Sir Duncan Cameron ordered Colonel Weare to march with the division under his command from the Waetotara to the Patea river, leaving a detachment of 200 men under Major Rocke, 18th Regiment, to occupy a post on the left bank of the Waetotara, for the purpose of securing a passage across that river, and keeping the communication open with Wanganui.

On the morning of the 13th, Colonel Weare was ordered, in the absence of Brigadier-General Waddy, who was incapacitated for duty by a severe fall from his horse, to move, with 1273 officers and men, up the right bank of the Patea towards the village of Kakaramea. The General was present with the troops.

After marching some two and a half miles, the right flank of the line of march became commanded by a range of hills covered with thick fern, affording a very strong position, and on which the advance guard skirmishers discovered the enemy skilfully posted.

The advance guard, under Major Butler, 57th, was then ordered to change direction to the right, and additional companies of that regiment were thrown into skirmishing order to prolong a line to the left, so as to turn the enemy's right, and keep him from escaping to the village of Manutahi, in the direction of the ultimate advance.

The cavalry was also drawn to that flank. While this was being done, the attention of the enemy was directed to their left flank by a few rounds from the artillery.

The whole line then advanced on the Maori position, supported by the 68th Regiment, with the 50th Regiment in reserve. The enemy clung tenaciously to his strong position, and many casualties must have occurred had he not seen that he was being outflanked, and his retreat about to be cut off by the cavalry. He then gave way, and was followed up over most difficult ground, consisting of a series of hills, with deep swamps running along their base, until the village of Kakaramea was reached.

It being impossible for the artillery and cavalry to follow the enemy over this ground, they were ordered to resume the original direction of march, supported by the 50th Regiment, and threaten the village of Kakaramea on the left, while the remainder of the troops pushed on across the swamps to take it in front. The enemy, seeing this disposition, did not rally to defend it. Twenty-seven dead bodies were found, three wounded (who afterwards died), and two prisoners were secured. Had there been time to search the extensive swamps, many more might have been discovered; and it was understood that the enemy's loss amounted to about sixty killed and wounded.

The British loss was small in this fight at Patea—one man was killed and three men severely wounded—which was attributed to the arrangements made for turning the right flank of the enemy before advancing upon him. In this, the General being present, Colonel Weare derived the benefit of his advice and experience.

The name of Sergeant O'Connor, 57th Regiment, was brought prominently to the notice of the General for dash and soldierlike bearing.

Major Greaves, 70th Regiment, Deputy Assistant - Quartermaster - General, was conspicuous, as on all other occasions, for his energy and daring; also Captain Leach, 50th Regiment, Deputy Assistant-Adjutant-General, had thanks especially accorded to him.   Staff Field-

Surgeon Home, whose anxiety to be ready to aid any wounded led him to be always up with the advance, and his kind attention to and sympathy for the wounded in this Wanganui campaign, was much felt by the soldiers.

On the morning of the 14th of March, on the return of the transport which had been sent back to the Patea river the previous evening for provisions, the field force again advanced, at ten A.M., over an open country covered with fern, but without roads, and much intersected with ravines, to the village of Manutahi, which is situated at the edge of a dense bush, and through a portion of which the troops had to pass before reaching the village. Such was the labour of making cuttings and passing the transport over the ravines, that, although the distance was only six miles, the rear guard with the last carts did not reach camp till eleven o'clock at night.

Manutahi was a large and important settlement of the Maoris, judging by the amount of crops growing, which was far in excess of those found at Rangiawhia; and the loss of so much food was now a serious blow to the natives: 200 tons of potatoes were collected, besides other crops, and secured.

The Wanganui campaign was necessarily attended with much labour and fatigue, and now at the beginning of the New Zealand winter it was time to establish posts and secure what had been gained by the steady advance to the west coast.

The heroic Wolfe, the evening before his final battle on the plains of Abraham, Quebec, is said to have sung his favourite soldier's song, " How stands the glass around?" It concludes thus—

> " 'Tis but in vain
> (I mean not to upbraid you, boys),
> 'Tis but in vain
> For soldiers to complain :
> Should next campaign
> Send us to Him who made us, boys,
> We're free from pain;
> But should we remain,
> A bottle and kind landlady cures all again."

CHAPTER XV.

GENERAL SIR DUNCAN CAMERON, from the camp
at Waetotara, wrote to the Military Secretary in
England, General Forster, K.H., that he wished
to be relieved of the command of the troops in
New Zealand. He made this application with
extreme reluctance, but his health was impaired
by the arduous and harassing duties which had
devolved upon him since the commencement

s

of the war (and also at the close of the previous
war), and particularly by the great heat of the
two last summers, which were passed under
canvas in the field; and thus he solicited that
another officer might be appointed to relieve
him.   H.R.H. the Field-Marshal Commanding-
in-Chief, highly appreciating the many valuable
services rendered by this distinguished officer—
as did the Secretary of State for War—and
regretting the cause of his asking to be relieved, yet, in anticipation of the speedy cessa-
tion of hostilities, consent was not withheld
to the General's application.

Commanding the troops in Scotland in 1861
(an object of great ambition to many Scotch
officers), he had been taken from this position to
proceed to New Zealand.   Continuing to be
highly in favour with the authorities, he was
appointed, when he returned to England,
to Military Commissions, and then became
Governor of the Royal Military College, being
esteemed one of the best read and most accomplished officers in the British army.

The troops under Sir Duncan Cameron had advanced to the Waingoro river; he had established posts there, and at the Waetotara and Patea rivers, at Kakaramea, and at Manawapo. The supply of the posts by sea was very precarious. Stores were disembarked from a steamer only on one occasion; trying to discharge a second steamer, the lives of four soldiers and two sailors were lost by the upsetting of a surf-boat. Of four surf-boats, one had become entirely disabled and two seriously damaged. The sea on the west coast of New Zealand is very wild at times, rolling in huge billows against the rocky cliffs or sandy beach.

General Cameron, having only a moveable force of 800 men, could not establish more military posts than he did; and posts were of course necessary for securing what had been acquired by conquest in Waikato, Tauranga, and Wanganui. The Colonial Secretary declined to send any reinforcements to New Zealand, since it was desired to recall five regiments, and reduce the force as soon as

s 2

possible. The same opinion was expressed at the War Office.

The labours of the Commissariat were at this time very great, to supply the troops with fresh meat and bread; but their exertions under Deputy Commissary-General Strickland were unremitting to provide what was required, under great difficulties of transport, &c. Mr. Strickland found the pack-saddle of the Otago diggers the best—high above the withers of the horse, while the sides of it rested firmly on the horse. Compressed forage was supplied at first in too large packets, each of 132 lbs.; and it was recommended that they should not exceed 120 lbs., and be long and flat, so as to be carried on pack-horses.

Another surf-boat was upset at the mouth of the Waingoro river, and more men were drowned.

A party of natives had visited the house of Mr. Hewett, on the frontier of the Wanganui settlement, and murdered him. He was an old resident, and much respected in the neighbourhood. The house was the most exposed of any in the out-settlements ; but he declined to have a picket stationed there from a neighbouring redoubt at Mussens, under the impression that it would invite attack. His body was found decapitated, and the head taken away.

The friendly chief, Rio, was also murdered.

Military posts were established at Te Namu, fifty miles south of New Plymouth, at Pukearhoe, the White Cliffs, thirty-five miles north of it, and garrisoned by troops of the Taranaki command.

At Tauranga, on the 28th of May, 1865, Wiremu Tamehana (William Thompson), and other chiefs, came to Brigadier-General Carey and tendered their submission to British authority. When the Brigadier met Thompson, the latter dismounted from his horse, came forward uncovered, and grounded his taiaha, or carved chief's spear, and shook hands. They then proceeded with the other chiefs to where the British flag was flying, and signed a covenant of peace.

William Thompson made these requests,—that a Commission should be appointed to inquire into his conduct and character, which he said had been much maligned; and that he wished to see the face of the Governor again. A gentleman I knew and corresponded with in New Zealand, Mr. George Graham, and for whom I have great esteem for his highly judicious manner of dealing with the Maoris (and assisted on this occasion by Mr. Dehar), was the means of rendering this important service to the colony,—the submission of the chiefs at Tauranga. He deserved every honour the Government could confer on him.

The translation of the convention signed by William Thompson and other chiefs in presence of Brigadier-General Carey was—

"We consent that the laws of the Queen be laws for the (Maori) King, to be a protection for us all for ever and ever. This is the sign of making peace, my coming here, to the presence of my fighting friend (Hoa-riri) General Carey."

A number of the natives in the Taranaki

came in and surrendered themselves to Colonel
Warre and to Mr. Parris at Stony river.

There was a misfortune in Taranaki. Some
commissariat bullocks had gone astray, and
Colonel Colville allowed four mounted men to go
a short way into the bush to look for them; but
seeing some horses and cows in the distance
they gave chase, and were joined by a sergeant
and five privates, 43rd Light Infantry, unarmed
and without orders, for the purpose of wild pig
hunting. When leading away a calf, they were
surprised and attacked by a dozen mounted
Maoris. All wonderfully escaped except two, a
private of the 43rd and one of the mounted
company; the rest returned singly and in pairs
to camp. The body of the mounted man was
found, but not the 43rd soldier.

It was now determined by the Colonial
Government to form a military settlement of
120 officers and soldiers north of the Waitara
river, Taranaki, and also a settlement of friendly
natives there, with block houses for defence.

The Maoris in the Taranaki, having made

repeated attacks on the post at Warea, about twenty-six miles south of New Plymouth, Colonel Warre directed Lieut. - Colonel Colville, 43rd Light Infantry, to proceed from New Plymouth, on the 29th of July, with a flying column to punish the enemy, and drive him out of the bush.

The force consisted of 213 officers and men, 43rd and 70th Regiments, and a gun detachment of Royal Artillery, with a 6-pounder Armstrong gun. After passing Warea, at Kapoiaiai, the force was divided, and Brevet-Major Russell, 57th, took charge of one-half: this column turned inland, and Colonel Colville continued along the coast for some distance. Thus there was a combined movement to surprise the enemy in the bush. The gun was left at Warea. Great difficulties were experienced in making way through the bush, for the want of a good guide, by Colonel Colville's party. Major Russell first encountered the enemy about six miles from the beach.

He posted pickets on four conical hills, sent

forward Captain Cay with sixty men to reconnoitre a smoke observed in the bush, who
creeping forward, a collection of twenty wharrés
was seen. Captain Cay immediately fixed
bayonets, and charged among the huts, and
took the natives quite by surprise, and slew a
number of them.

Lieutenant Tylden, 70th, was severely
wounded in two places, in the hand and cheek,
leading on his company.

Soon after, Captain Cay rejoined Major Russell, bringing with him two men and a woman
prisoners. The Maoris rallied, and opened a
heavy fire on the party, the natives firing with
great precision and steadiness, and causing
casualties among the troops; the Maoris also
suffering. The natives continued to follow the
party, which made several stands to keep them
in check. Lieutenant Bully, 70th, commanding
the rear guard, was mortally wounded through
the stomach.

Colonel Colville, hearing the heavy firing
from Major Russell's party, came up with it

after its attack on the Okea wharrés, and the enemy was driven off. This was on the 2nd of August.

On the 3rd of August, Colonel Colville returned to the bush to complete the destruction of the village of Okea, which Captain Cay had been unable to accomplish the previous day, owing to the small number of his men and the determined resistance of the enemy.

The casualties were one officer, Lieutenant Bully, 70th, killed; and one officer, Lieutenant Tylden, 70th, severely wounded; four privates killed, and five severely wounded. It was believed twenty or thirty of the enemy were killed and wounded. It was a sharp bush fight.

Major Russell and Captain Cay were highly commended by Colonel Colville for this affair near Warea. Captains the Hon. A. G. Harris and Talbot, 43rd Light Infantry, were of great service in skirmishing; and Lieutenant Longley, 43rd, commanding the advance guard, found the track when a native guide refused to go on. On getting under fire, Captain F. Mace, of the

Taranaki Militia, accompanied the party, and
was of great assistance. Surgeon Turner, 43rd,
was of great service to the wounded.

Major-General Trevor Chute, on the departure
of Sir Duncan Cameron from Melbourne on the
25th of August, assumed the command of the
forces in the Australian Colonies and New
Zealand, and arrived at Auckland on the 27th
of August.

Instructions were issued for the departure of
the 65th Regiment, who certainly had become
acclimatised in New Zealand, and had done
excellent service there in the seventeen years of
colonial experience. The 70th Regiment proceeded from the Taranaki to Napier, to aid in
the defence of the province of Hawkes Bay
against the Hauhau fanatics; and 500 of the
colonial forces were withdrawn from Wanganui
and landed at Opotiki, about seventy miles
south-east of Tauranga, with a view to punish
the murderers of the Rev. Mr. Volkner and Mr.
Falloon. This was a dreadful affair, which will
be shortly related.

Mr. Volkner was a Prussian Protestant missionary, and a member of the English Church in New Zealand for some years. He was a man of peculiarly mild and gentle disposition, at the same time zealous in his holy calling. His station was at Opotiki, on the Bay of Plenty, east coast. Gradually he so improved the tribe among whom he dwelt and laboured, that they became quiet and orderly, and so esteemed him that they built for him a church and dwelling-house. Some of his people became excited and violent when the Waikato campaign began, and it was thought prudent to remove Mrs. Volkner to Auckland. Unfortunately he returned to his station, where he was visited by a party of the Hauhau fanatics from the Taranaki, breathing murder against the Pakeha, and carrying with them the cooked head of a white man, and a soldier also as a prisoner.

Mr. Volkner returned to Opotiki on the 1st of March ; accompanying him was another missionary, the Rev. Mr. Grace. They came in a

small schooner called the "Eclipse," Captain
Levy.

Mr. Grace I had known under peculiar circumstances. One day in 1862, in cruising
about alone on the fern ridges of the Waikato
(I was on good terms with the natives about
there, having opened a trade with them with
our people, and had no occasion to fear them),
I saw a white man and a young woman walking
along a bush track, with a few Maoris carrying
packs. This was Mr. Grace and his good-look-
ing daughter, retreating from his station at
the Taupo lake. I took them to our camp and
entertained them, and they proceeded on their
way to Auckland.

As soon as the "Eclipse" anchored at Opotiki,
the Hauhaus boarded her, and made prisoners of
the two missionaries, confining them on shore.
Mr. Grace said they spent a dreadful night of
suspense, and next day, in the afternoon, twenty
armed men came and took out Mr. Volkner.
They said he was to die. They then performed
some wild ceremonies at a flag-staff, and taking

him to his own church, they deprived him of his coat and waistcoat, then took him to a tree, where there was a rope thrown over a branch. He saw now what was intended, and knelt in prayer to his Maker. His cruel murderers then threw a noose round his neck, and ran him up to the tree, and left him hanging for an hour. He was then cut down and decapitated, his eyes taken out, and his body thrown aside, but it was afterwards buried by Captain Levy and some of the natives.

My poor friend, Mr. Grace, thought every day would be his last, till the 16th of March, when, H.M.S. "Eclipse" coming to Opotiki, Captain Levy, at the risk of his life, took off Mr. Grace in his boat to the man-of-war, and he most thankfully escaped.

Not content with the murder of Mr. Volkner, in July, when Mr. Fulloon, a half-caste interpreter, arrived at Wakatane in a schooner owned by natives, but with an English crew, the Hauhaus boarded her, murdered Mr. Fulloon in his berth, and the crew, and burnt the vessel.

Strange, they spared Mr. White, a trader, and a half-caste boy.

When a party of the 14th Regiment were at Parakino, a redoubt on the Wanganui river, in the end of 1865, a large wharré was built there to serve to dance in or for a theatre, and the friendly Maoris there occasionally lent the soldiers clothing to perform their parts. On one occasion the Maoris gave a *haka*, or war dance, as an interlude, one of their chiefs, Reneti, leading. As they grew excited in their performance, so did a number of the Maoris among the audience, and, jumping on the stage, they joined the rest in their tremendous stamping and contortions. The soldiers gave them immense applause, which was much relished by the Maoris.

The natives were on the most friendly terms with the soldiers, often gave them, without asking for payment, potatoes, fruit, and vegetables, and got in return an occasional glass of rum, or an invitation to eat "a bit of dinner" in a tent.

There were athletic games held, and swimming races; in a *short* race the Maoris beat the soldiers, and a Maori saved the life of a drowning soldier.

On the south-west coast, Brigadier-General Waddy had sent Mr. Charles Broughton, an interpreter, well known to the Maoris, with offers of peace. He was enticed into a pah where a flag of truce was hoisted; he never returned—he, too, was murdered.

His Excellency Sir George Grey had set his heart on the capture of the strong Wereroa pah, situated on high and commanding ground, up the Waetotara river. It was a sort of Bhurtpore to the Maoris, and supposed to be impregnable, and defiant for the Pakeha.

The Wanganuis, flushed with their success against the Hauhaus, were anxious to assist in taking Wereroa.

Sir Duncan Cameron had not been in favour of commencing siege operations against the Wereroa pah in winter rains, but intended that the post at Nukumaru should be used for observation, and for collecting siege materials, and then to make the attempt to carry the pah when the proper season arrived ; meanwhile an opportunity might occur to surprise the pah, or the natives might evacuate it, fearing the effect of an assault.

Sir Duncan Cameron, before he left New Zealand (and Sir George Grey being desirous of ascertaining if the road was clear round the south-west coast) directed Colonel Warre, C.B., to march with a force from Opunaki to meet Colonel Weare from Waingongora, and to make a reconnaissance between the two points. This was done, and the two detachments met about half-way without having seen an enemy. The distance between the two outposts was about twenty-four miles.

The Wereroa pah stood about 300 feet above the wooded banks of the Waetotara. There were woods, and broken country, and occasional swamps all round, quite a picture of New Zealand scenery.

The front of the pah, on its high plateau,

T

formed as it were the base of a triangle, one end
of which rested on the Koie stream, the other
on the Waetotara river.   On the right bank of
the Koie was a precipitous wooded ridge, somewhat higher than that on which the pah stood.
The right bank of the Koie stream then afforded
excellent cover for riflemen, and commanded a
great part of the pah itself.

The front of the pah stood at the head of a
gentle slope, which fell gradually away from
the pah, for a distance of more than 1000 yards,
when the ground began again gradually to rise.
The front face of the pah was very strongly
fortified with palisading and rifle-pits.*   It was
not expected that a force would advance to
attack the pah by the precipitous valleys on its
flanks, where the cliffs formed the chief defence.

Sir George Grey determined to occupy by
surprise the heights commanding the pah, and

---

* In that excellent work by Captain A. V. Boguslawski, trans-
lated by Colonel Lumley Graham, and entitled ' Tactical Deduc-
tions from the War of 1870–71,' it is said " The rifle pit is by far
the simplest field work, and that best suited to the tactics of the
present day."

by a force, if possible, strong enough to repel any sortie from the pàh (which would be at the same time threatened in front), and also strong enough · to repulse or capture any reinforcements that might be coming up.

Brigadier-General Waddy had arranged to establish a post of 400 men of the regular troops about 900 yards from the fortress, to afford Her Majesty's Colonial forces and the native allies that moral support · they were certain to derive from the presence of British troops in front of the place. He also ordered a detachment of artillery to co-operate in front, to breach and shell the works, if necessary.

The Colonial troops were 25 Wanganui Cavalry, 139 Forest Rangers, 109 Native Contingent, 200 efficient friendly natives, and several old warriors—total 473.

A post at Pipiriki, commanded by Captain Brassey, was placed in a very critical position— threatened with attack by a large body of natives; but until Wereroa fell, it was impossible to detach a party to assist Captain

Brassey, so no time was to be lost in trying to gain possession of Wereroa.

Sir George Grey taking the direction of the operations, determined to occupy the heights round the pah, to shut in its defenders, and to harass them with rifle and artillery fire. Mr. Parris, the interpreter, communicated to the native allies the intentions of the Governor, and had them on the alert on the morning of the 20th of July.

Lieut.-Colonel Trevor, with 100 men of the 14th Regiment, arrived early on the morning of the 20th, and pitched his tents in front of the pah, about 1300 yards from it, and between the camps of the native allies and the Forest Rangers ; Captain Noblett, 18th Royal Irish, with 100 men, also arrived on the ground to co-operate, and pitched his tents in rear of the 14th.

At half-past twelve, the Colonial and native forces, under Major Rooke's command, paraded out of sight of the pah, and moved off north to the Karaka heights, by a path concealed from the view of the pah. It rained heavily, which, though inconvenient to the men marching, helped to conceal the well-devised movement. The supplies of food were short, yet there were no complaints, and all were anxious to execute what had been assigned to them to attempt— they were " strong and of good courage."

The Forest Rangers were under the command of Captain George, the Native Contingent under Captain MacDonell, the friendly natives under their several chiefs ; and the whole, under Major Rooke, reached the Karaka heights by ravines and broken and wooded ground, by half-past six o'clock P.M., after dark.

From the time the Colonial forces left (with the exception of a few friendly natives) the regular troops, 200 in number, under the command of Lieut.-Colonel Trevor, were the only force in front of the pah. Sir George Grey afterwards said, " Without the presence of this force, the operations could not have been carried on. Nothing could have surpassed the zeal and energy of Lieut.-Colonel Trevor;

and to his cordial co-operation and advice on several occasions, much of the success which followed must be attributed. The officers and men of the regular troops all exhibited the greatest alacrity and interest in what was going on . . . . without their presence, and without the cordial energetic assistance which they gave, nothing could have been done."

Of course there was great risk in dividing the force, but appearances were well kept up, and the natives in the pah were deceived, all the tents being left pitched in view of the pah. Captain Brassey's critical position at Pipiriki required the risk to be run. But if the enemy had suspected that only 200 men were in their front, as at Nukumaru, they might have sallied out in great numbers, and tried the mettle of the 14th and 18th in a bloody conflict.

In the course of the night Major Rooke asked the Chief Haimona to send spies to a kainga or village near; they reported that there was no one there : but not satisfied with that, the Major detached a party under Captain McDonell at half-past four in the morning to the kainga, who surprised and captured a reinforcement for the pah, and made fifty prisoners, fifty stand of arms, and two kegs of ammunition. Great credit was due for this to Captain McDonell and his men.

At daybreak on the morning of the 21st, rifle-shots from the Karaka heights into Wereroa pah wakened its defenders; they were taken by surprise, and evidently fell into confusion, not expecting an attack from the north side.

The native chiefs left in camp with Colonel Trevor became naturally anxious at their critical position; to reassure them he sent for fifty more men of the 14th to Nukumaru, and for fifty more, 18th, to Waetotara. The 200 regulars expected from Wanganui had not arrived, but the operations went on, Major Rooke to harass the enemy in the pah by day and laying ambuscades at night—Colonel Trevor to make a sham attack on the pah in front, to enable Major Rooke to take the Parima village on his side, and the friendly natives occupying the ground on the west side of the Waetotara river.

At sunset the pickets falling in and marching to the front, led the enemy to suppose the troops were forming for a night attack; the garrison was seen to be in confusion, and running about for shelter from the rifle-shots from the heights.

Major Rocke, 18th, arriving in command of a party from the Waetotara, reported to Colonel Trevor he had seen, with a telescope, natives descending the cliffs and precipitous banks with packs, and escaping by the only outlet from the pah. At ten o'clock, 21st, Major Rooke ascertained from a native scout that the pah was evacuated, and he had the satisfaction of writing Sir George Grey, " The Wereroa is yours." It was immediately taken possession of by the friendly natives, and then garrisoned by Colonel Trevor and the 14th detachment.

Great credit was due to all engaged in the capture of the Wereroa pah. Sir George Grey planned the attack, and the regular troops eagerly aided him (Lieut.-Colonel Trevor was afterwards rewarded with the C.B.), and to Major Rooke, Captain George, Captain and

Adjutant Ross, and to the native Chiefs Haimona, Te Kepa, Epiha, Aperaniko, and Karehana, great praise was accorded.

His Excellency Sir George Grey, K.C.B., I first knew at the Cape of Good Hope, when as Captain Grey, on his way with Lieutenant Lushington, he was proceeding to explore the north-west coast of Australia, at Sharks Bay, for the Government. He was handed over to me by my distinguished Chief Sir Benjamin d'Urban (whose private secretary and A.D.C. I was) to fit out with supplies for his expedition, on which he was dangerously wounded by a spear. He had obtained first-class honours at the senior department Royal Military College, and gave so much satisfaction to the Colonial Secretaries of State, that he was appointed Governor, in succession, of South Australia, New Zealand, the Cape of Good Hope, and New Zealand a second time. His public services fully entitled him to be called a very distinguished " man of the time."

CHAPTER XVI.

Skirmishing in Taranaki—Captain Close is killed—Dangerous adventure of three officers of the 14th Regiment—Colonel Colville's ambuscade—He is wounded—Reception of the Native Contingent at Wanganui — General Chute prepares to conduct a campaign against the Hauhaus — The force organised—Okotuku taken — Difficulties of the assault on Putahi pah — Smart action at Otapawa — Colonel Hassard killed—Successes against the Hauhaus—Preparations for a bush march round Mount Egmont to New Plymouth—Difficulties of the undertaking—Labour and privations encountered—Horseflesh used—The force received with distinction —End of the service of the regular troops—Proclamation of peace.

SUBSEQUENT to the fall of the Wereroa pah, some skirmishes took place in Taranaki. A party under Captain Close, 43rd Regiment, of one subaltern, Ensign O'Brien, two sergeants, one bugler, and fifty-one rank and file, went from the camp at Werea to patrol the country on the 28th July. They were guided by Jim, a Maori, and came upon a large number of the enemy on a hill,

who commenced gesticulating and shouting
" Pai Mariri ! " The party advanced on the
Maoris in skirmishing order, and were received
with a heavy volley, by which Captain Close
was mortally wounded through the left eye, and
a private was killed—this was at Konga-Kumi-
Kumi. The natives firing in front also tried
to outflank the detachment; two of the men
were wounded, also the guide Jim : bayonets
were charged by Ensign O'Brien, and the enemy
was dispersed. Sergeants Horley and Phelan
behaved extremely well on this occasion ; and
Bugler Croghan remained under a shower of
bullets to guard the body of Captain Close, and
behaved with such courage that it was considered he had earned the decoration of the
Victoria Cross. Assistant-Surgeon Grant cared
for the wounded.

On the 24th of August three officers of the
14th Regiment, stationed at the Wereroa pah,
went down the gully on the left of the pah for
the purpose of tracking some footsteps, which
had been seen early in the day, of natives who

had come up the night before. The officers imprudently continued their search to the village of Perikamo, 400 yards in rear of the pah, and then went round the spur of the hill, 300 yards, and set fire to an old wharré. On their return Captain Bryce (a relative) wandered towards the bank of the river for game, when shots were fired at him from its banks and from the bush on his other flank.

The officers retreated towards the pah, but were all wounded : they were Captain Bryce, Lieutenant and Adjutant Butler, and Ensign Symonds; also two soldiers, Carey and Green, who went to their assistance.

Ensign Symonds threw himself into the river to swim across, and was followed by two natives; he managed to hide himself in the bush till assistance was sent him. Lieutenant Butler owed his life, as he said, to Captain Bryce, who by his coolness, and armed with a fowling piece, was able to keep at bay the natives, who were gaining fast on them. Though of course it was tedious to be shut up in a pah, yet this affair shewed the danger of wandering from one's post while hostilities were still being carried on.

During the Maori war a sergeant of the 14th Regiment had a disagreeable night adventure. He was on outpost duty ; and on coming back from patrol he found that his blanket had disappeared. As the night was not warm, he went in search of a covering, and seeing some men in blankets lying on the ground, he laid down beside them, and gradually drew off a couple of their blankets to make himself comfortable. After dosing for some time, and the moon breaking through the clouds, he found he was lying among some dead Maoris, and of course he suddenly left his silent bedfellows.

In the Taranaki, on the 22nd of October, a party of the 43rd left the Werea camp at a quarter past two A.M., under the command of Lieut.-Colonel Colville, to lay an ambush for the hostile natives at a place called Ngakumikumi, about three miles from camp. The force was concealed in an old pah. Captain Mace left Werea at seven A.M. with his mounted men, to draw the enemy towards the ambuscade. Lieut.-Longley, with twenty-five men detached in front, opened fire upon a party of natives coming along the path, who, immediately taking advantage of the cover afforded by a gully, returned the fire briskly. Another party of natives advanced in skirmishing order towards the hill-side, occupied by Colonel Colville, and heavy firing took place from both sides. The native fire slackened by degrees, when the natives retired. Colonel Colville was seriously wounded in the thigh, a sergeant was killed, and two men were dangerously wounded. Captain Harris, 43rd, brought in the party.

On the 25th of November, 1865, the Native Contingent who had gone to the east coast for active service, and to avenge the murder of Mr. Volkner and others of our countrymen there, returned to Wanganui, and were received with every honour. They had previously fought well in defence of that settlement. Walter Buller, Esq., Resident Magistrate, Major von Tempski, Forest Rangers, and others, went on

board the "Storm Bird" to welcome the native
allies; His Honour, Dr. Featherston, the Superintendent and now the Agent-general for
New Zealand in London, met them with congra-
tulations. The natives esteemed him as a father
to them.

Major-General Chute, in compliance with the
desire of the Governor, now being prepared to
make a campaign against the hostile natives,
the Hauhaus (the inveterate enemies of the
Pakehas, who refused offers of peace), between Wanganui and New Plymouth, organised the following force, and marched out of
Wanganui for Waetotara on the 30th of December.

Royal Artillery	33
Her Majesty's 14th Regiment	107
Native Contingent	286
Forest Rangers	45

The Native Contingent joined with women
among them, who carry packs, cook, and fight
on occasion, and utterly despise those of their
people who are backward in action ; but ladies
generally do this everywhere.

The transport consisted of forty-five drays, two horses to each.

On the 2nd of January, 1866, his Honour Dr. Featherston, the Superintendent of Wellington, joined the camp at Waetotara, along with some native chiefs, and continued during the campaign with the troops, and was of the greatest service to the cause in which they were engaged.

As a commencement, a party of the contingent went out and captured thirty-two horses, and brought them into camp.

On the 3rd of January, Lieut.-Colonel Trevor joined the force, with 132 officers and men of the 14th Regiment, also detachments of the 18th Regiment joined under Major Rocke, and of the 50th under Captain Johnstone. The Native Contingent, under Major McDonell, next attacked the Hauhaus in the village of Ohine Motu, and drove them out of it, and pursued them for three miles beyond.

The march of General Chute's force was then directed on Okotuku, some natives from which had waylaid and murdered some white men. It was a palisaded village, with well-fenced cultivation all round it. The native contingent and Forest Rangers skirmished round it, and Captain Vivian was ordered to charge with a party of the 14th : they did this in good style, Lieutenant Keogh and Ensign Callwell, the subalterns ; and the natives, after resisting, fled from their pah, sliding down the banks in rear of it, with the assistance of ladders of supplejack. Lieutenant Keogh and three privates, 14th Regiment, were wounded. Six bodies of the natives were found, and their wounded were carried off. The native contingent celebrated their success with a *haka* or war-dance by moonlight.

The next enterprise was the attack on a very strong pah—Putahi, on a plateau, supported by precipitous spurs, and cleft by deep forest gullies. The approach to it was favourable for ambuscades to receive an attacking force.

At three A.M. on the 7th, the General proceeded with about 700 officers and men of all arms from their camp, which was 1500 yards from

U

the pah, and making their way in silence and
darkness across the valley, ascended the ridges
of Putahi. The Native Contingent, knowing
the ground, led the way, under Major Mac
Donell and Captain Kemp, followed by Major
von Tempski, a valuable partisan officer, and
his Rangers. General Chute and his staff,
Major Pitt, and Captain Leach headed the
column of regulars by an exceedingly steep and
rough path.

The last ascent to the pah was almost perpendicular, but the forest screen, and aided by
the branches of the trees, made climbing possible.
The plateau of the pah gained, Major Mac
Donell was sent round to the rear of the pah,
and Major von Tempski opened fire in front at
300 yards; the Hauhau flag was then hoisted,
and a war-dance performed by the garrison, 200
strong, to get up their courage.

Young Mr. Campbell, of the Rangers, exposing himself, fell wounded, and the firing
between the Rangers and the pah continued for
an hour. General Chute now drew up his

regulars to rush at the pah, and cut down part
of the palisading with hatchets and bill-hooks—
14th in the centre, 18th on the right, and 50th
on the left. Bayonets were fixed, and with a
cheer the pah was entered. A private, Michael
Coffey, 14th, hauled down the Hauhau flag, and
presented it to his commanding officer, Colonel
Trevor. Malcolm, a Ranger, was shot behind
Major Von Tempski, and some of the Contingent
were struck. The enemy fled into the bush, and
were pursued by the Native Contingent, and ten
fell, besides fifteen killed in and about the pah.

Before the pah was burnt, several books and
papers which had belonged to Mr. Hewitt (who
was murdered on his farm) were found ; also the
harness of the horses of the carrier Arbon, who
was waylaid and murdered on his way to Wanganui ; and a paper in Maori arranging a plan
for attacking Wanganui at an early day. A
valuable whaleboat was also found concealed on
the banks of the Wheneakura* river. Colonel
Weare intercepted a small party of fugitives

* Red soil.

from Putahi, killed one, wounded another, and made a third prisoner.

After a day's rest, the march was continued, the mouth of the Wheneakura was forded at low-water, and at the camp of Kakaramea the force was augmented by two six-pounder Armstrong guns, and two sergeants and 15 gunners of the Royal Artillery.

On the 11th of January, Lieut.-Colonel Hassard, 57th Regiment, joined with 120 men of his regiment; next day the march was to Ketemarae, a very strong pah. The camp was formed a mile from it, where Colonel Butler joined it.

At the large village of Taiporohenui stood a King's parliament house, 100 feet by 40, for runangas or conferences; this was burnt, and the cooked dinners of the Hauhaus were found there, consisting of beef, boiled potatoes, and native cabbage, &c., in abundance; also a butcher's shop, with scales and weights—an advance in civilisation. There were also herds of tame cattle in good condition, horses, pigs, and cultivated fields.

The stronghold of Otapawa was now reconnoitred. Like Putahi, it was considered impregnable and inaccessible to Europeans. It
was considered the most important position in
the Ngatiruanui country, and had never fallen
to an enemy. At two A.M., 18th of January, the
following force marched to attack it :—

Royal Artillery, with three guns, under Lieutenant Carre.
Her Majesty's 14th Regiment, 200 men, under Lieu^t.
Colonel Trevor.
Her Majesty's 57th Regiment, 180 men, under Lieut.-
Colonel Butler.
Forest Rangers, 36 men, under Major Von Tempski.
Native Contingent, 200 men, under Ensign MacDonell.

It was ascertained that artillery could play on
the pah from a neighbouring height, and this
was put in execution with effect. The Native
Contingent were ordered to the rear of the pah,
while the General attacked in front. The 57th
led, followed by the Rangers and the 14th.
Three shots from the Armstrongs had called
forth no reply from the Hauhaus, an unusual
thing, and the pah seemed abandoned. It was
not so. Colonel Butler, within 200 yards of
the pah, saw the rifle-pits in rear of the pali-

sading thickly lined with black heads (the garrison was 200 strong), and a bush at right angles to the pah was also full of Maoris. There was silence but no hesitation, and the General gave the word, " 57th, advance ! Rangers, clear the bush ! "—They went off at double quick, as did the 14th, who extended in front of the pah firing. The Rangers got to the rear of the pah. The 57th suffered severely from the cross-fire on the right ; and Colonel Butler then led his men to the left and entered the pah with the Rangers in rear. The 14th, when also inside the pah, suffered from a fire from wicker-work platforms on trees round the pah, till the occupants of them were disposed of.

The Hauhaus lost fifty men killed. The loss of the force was Colonel Hassard and nine men killed, and Lieutenant Swanson, 14th, and fourteen men wounded, including Major MacDonell, the brave commander of the Native Contingent.

Ketemarai was next to be attacked, but it fell without resistance, as did several other pahs and hamlets, which were burnt in sight of the snowy

peak of the magnificent Mount Egmont. The
Hauhaus were evidently cowed by the fate of
Otawapa.

MOUNT EGMONT.

General Chute's "ready" mode of attacking
pahs was this. There was usually an open
plateau in front of the pahs; he brought up his
men there to the edge of the bush, and when
his line and supports and natives in reserve were
all ready, he made his bugler sound a single

G; the men advanced from under cover, and
on the double G being given, a rush was made
at the pah, hatchets were drawn from the
belts of the men, the withes of the outer fence
were suddenly cut, the palisading broken
through, and the pah stormed with cheering,
" in the smoke."

All the principal villages and positions of the
Hauhaus up to and within reach of the head-
quarters camp at Ketemarai having been
destroyed and the enemy scattered with heavy
loss, General Chute proposed, in accordance
with Sir George Grey's instructions, to continue his march immediately towards New
Plymouth, by the bush-track round the east
side of Mount Egmont. This was a novel and
remarkable undertaking, and proved that white
soldiers could not be stopped by the difficulties
of bush-ranging.

General Chute could get no reliable information regarding the track, so he embarked on the
undertaking with considerable anxiety, and
undertook it to fulfil the Governor's desire to

produce a salutary effect on the native mind.
The distance from Ketemarai to Mataitawa,
Taranaki, was fifty-four miles, and it took nine
days to accomplish this, always on the move for
ten hours daily. Twenty-one rivers had to be
crossed, and ninety gullies with precipitous
banks, and working parties were constantly in
advance, cutting down trees and clearing the
track of supplejack, &c., and making stairs of
tree fern logs and pickets up steep banks to
admit of the passage of the pack animals. The
weather, which had been fine for two days,
changed to continuous rain, which increased the
difficulties in crossing gullies, and necessitated
the construction of corduroy roads over swamps,
which might otherwise have been impracticable.

It was on the 17th of January, 1866, that
General Chute commenced his hazardous enter-
prise. He left his camp at Ketemarai at four
A.M. with 424 men of all ranks, 14th, 18th, 57th
Regiments and Royal Artillery, also fifty-four
Forest Rangers, and sixty-eight Native Contin-
gent with their veteran chief—Hori Kingi. The

transport consisted of sixty-seven pack-horses and
twenty-four riding-horses. The Major-General
rode in front, and on his staff were Colonel R.
Carey, C.B., Deputy Adjutant-General; Lieutenant-Colonel Gamble, C.B., Deputy Quartermaster - General; Major Pitt, Acting Military
Secretary; Captain Scott, Aide - de - Camp;
Deputy Commissary - General Strickland, the
head of the Commissariat; Deputy Inspector-
General Gibbs, the head of the Medical Department; and the Rev. Mr. Collins, Chaplain.

The men carried a waterproof sheet, a blanket,
and a great coat each, and two days' supply of
biscuits. Mr. Strickland took five days' supply
of food, except for the Native Contingent, who
insisted on getting all their rations in advance,
the result of which will afterwards appear.

Clearing their way with axes, tomahawks,
bill-hooks, and spades, and encountering a few
Hauhaus and making prisoner a girl of twelve
years old, going with a small party to get arms
for a pah—nine and a half miles were accomplished the first day. The second day the bush

became more dense and difficult of passage, and, as also on the next day, a difficult march. The tree-fern was well adapted for forming footing for the horses in the swamps, and the halt was made on the bank of the Mahatawi river. As the loads on the commissariat horses became consumed, the General allowed the men's packs to be carried on them. On the 20th the weather became gloomy, and a deep leaden sky was seen through the dense foliage of the forest; but the men sang and joked, Colonel Gamble encouraging them in every possible way, and there was no depression in the men's minds, though there was now no meat rations, and no tents had been taken with the force. On the fifth day the camp was without food, a most anxious time.

Deputy Assistant-Commissary-General Price now volunteered to start for the Taranaki for supplies, and was accompanied by Captain Leach and Ensign McDonell and ten of the ablest men of the Native Contingent. The rain came down in torrents, and Mr. Price became so

exhausted that he was obliged to be left in a
blanket at the foot of a large tree, and Captain
Leach gave him his last wet biscuit to keep
him alive.   Next morning the rest of the party
reached Mataitawa, as did Mr. Price, with the assistance of some friendly natives who found him.

On the 21st of January, after working hard
at clearing the track and road-making all day,
officers and men employed under soaking rain
and exhausted at night, a horse was killed and
distributed as rations.   The heart was reserved
for the General.   As I found in Africa with the
zebras and quaggas, soup was the best way to
deal with horse-flesh; but the men tried steaks
and chops, roast and boiled also.

"I'm not going to eat any of that horse!"
said one man.—"By dad, ye'll be glad to get it,
my boy, before the morning," said another; and
so it was, the objector to horse-flesh rose in the
night and took a ration of it gladly.

The Contingent, raging with hunger, from
imprudently not husbanding their supplies,
bolted ahead to search for food.   On the 22nd

another horse was killed and eaten : Captain
Leach, to whom the greatest praise is due,
came in exhausted with fatigue after forty-
eight hours' hard work, but with men laden
with food.   On the sixth day Colonel Warre
pushed on supplies, and two fat bullocks, biscuits,
and groceries were joyfully received in camp ;
but the country was so difficult to traverse from
the continued rain, that only four or five miles
were made, the men wading ankle deep, in the
two following days. On the 25th of January
they were out of the forest, and on the 27th
made a triumphal entry into New Plymouth.

Here General Chute and his force were received
with every honour and distinction ; also when he
returned to Wellington, Sir George Grey entertained him at a public dinner, at which 200
persons were present. From Her Majesty he received the Knight Commander's Star of the Bath,
and Colonel Colville the C.B., and Major Pitt.

Of His Honour Dr. Featherston, Superintendent of Wellington, Sir Trevor Chute said in a
report to Sir George Grey, "It is hardly possible

for me to convey to your Excellency how much I feel indebted to Dr. Featherston, Superintendent of the Province of Wellington, for his able advice on all subjects connected with the Maoris. He accompanied me throughout the campaign,* sharing all our dangers and privations, and was present at every engagement and assault. I am particularly obliged to him for the zeal with which he has at all times laboured to obtain information of the movements and positions of the enemy, which it would have been impossible for me to acquire without his assistance."

The claim for a high distinction for this valuable public servant will no doubt be duly recognised and acknowledged.

The fighting of the regular troops was now at an end, and the red-coats were gradually embarked to leave the colony for Australia, for India, or for England. Some bloody conflicts took place between the Colonial forces and the Hauhaus, as at Pukemaire pah, where Captain Westrupp, Lieutenant Biggs, and Ensign Ross

* It may be called the Mount Egmont campaign.—J. E. A.

particularly distinguished themselves. Colonel Whitmore, late Military Secretary to Sir Duncan Cameron, was employed in various military capacities in the colony after the regulars had left.

In one of these encounters one of my late regiment, the 14th, Captain Buck, was killed, and Major Von Tempski, while storming a pah at Ngatuotimanu (Parrot's beak pah), was shot. Thus perished an active officer, a very intelligent man and very deeply regretted.

It would enlarge this work too much if I attempted to narrate the exploits of Her Majesty's Colonial forces subsequent to 1866, which were so highly creditable to them, and resulted in peace : so I must now close this history of the War in New Zealand from 1863 to 1866.

A Proclamation of Peace was issued by His Excellency Sir George Grey, and countersigned by his minister, The Honourable Frederick A. Weld, announcing to the natives of New Zealand that the war which commenced at Oakura was at an end ; that the Governor had taken up arms to protect the European settlements from destruction, and to punish those who refused to settle by peaceable means the difficulties which had arisen, but resorted to violence and plunged the country into war. Upon those tribes sufficient punishment had been inflicted: their war parties had been beaten, their strongholds captured, and so much of their lands confiscated as was thought necessary to deter them from again appealing to arms.

His Excellency declared that none would now be prosecuted for past offences, except the murderers of certain settlers, &c., who were enumerated (Mr. Volkner, Mr. Falloon, &c.); that certain native lands, which had been taken in Waikato, Taranaki, and Ngatiruanui, would be restored, and boundaries settled by commissioners; and that His Excellency would consult with the great chiefs how the Maori people could be represented in the General Assembly and help to make the laws which they had to obey.

All this was liberal, just, and fair.

Having served much in British Colonies, I know and appreciate their great value and

importance to the Mother Country, and I much
regard the colonists, our own people, our equals,
and who ought at all times to be highly esteemed
for their energy and intelligence.

Loyalty to our gracious Sovereign will, I
trust, be ever preserved among them, and which,
as an old soldier, I imagine would be cemented
by seeing the British uniform wherever the
British flag was displayed.

APPENDIX.

I.

NEW ZEALAND STATISTICS.

THE noble colony of New Zealand was suffering in 1872-73, not from want of food or fuel, but from a want of labour to develop its great resources; its fertile soil requires hands to cultivate it, its flocks and herds require shepherds and herdsmen, its minerals require men to dig for them.

The New Zealand colonists are offering passages that will cost a good labourer no more on an average than his contribution of £5: whilst emigrant agents in England are trying to entice our workmen to Brazil, to the Argentine Republic, and even to Paraguay, a finer field for our people is offered, and better prospects of success are to be had, in the Britain of the south, New Zealand.

When the colony was in a disturbed state an extensive system of emigration could not be expected to be carried out towards it; but peace has reigned now for a considerable time, and no apprehension is to be entertained of interruption to the labours of the agriculturist or business of the trader. Post-office savings' banks and assurance offices in the colony are doing a large amount of business.

The Maoris, our late enemies, are making money, either cultivating their own lands or letting farms to white settlers at fair rents, or engaging themselves for the charge of flocks and herds.

Times seem to be entirely changed with them since the period when the writer was in New Zealand, and on one occasion, in the absence of Sir Gore Browne, was acting as Governor of the Colony. Then the anxiety of the Maoris to fight was great; so much so that a Maori came into Auckland with a bag of 300 gold pieces, collected among his people, and offered them to a trader for 600 boxes of copper caps—10s. a box; usual value 1s. 6d. Fortunately the bargain was not allowed to be concluded, and the Maori carried back his sovereigns. The money would now be laid out in a very different manner.

The European population may now amount to a quarter of a million; Maoris, say 40,000: 7,000 emigrants landed in 1872. Government land is sold by auction, at prices varying from 5s. to 40s. an acre. In the province of Auckland alone there are seventeen millions of acres; eleven millions of these still belong to the natives, and three millions to Government. "As beef and mutton can walk into market, they are more popular with the farmer than the more expensive transport of wheat." Agricultural wages are 5s. a day, or 15s. a week, with shelter and rations.

The bulk of the wool comes from the south island, where there are no Maoris, but a few employed as shepherds and cattle tenders.

The gold of New Zealand has been a great attraction

since 1860; it was then found in the south island, and worked. In 1868 the Thames gold-field, in the north island, was proved the richest in the colony. In the year ended on the 31st December, 1871, gold to the value of £1,888,708 was exported from Auckland, and the wages of a working miner were 50*s.* a week. In the south island the gold-fields of Westland have been thriving; they have sent home since 1860 about £6,500,000.

Coal is also abundant about the Waikato, &c., and was of great service during the war for the steamers.

From returns kindly furnished me by Falconer Larkworthy, Esq., managing director in London of the Bank of New Zealand, I find that, in the European population, the average for twelve years was one birth to every twenty-four and a half, and one death to every seventy-nine persons.

Shipping in 1871 :—

Vessels inwards	729
Tonnage	274,643
Vessels outwards	709
Tonnage	265,618
Imports in 1871, in value	£4,078,193
Exports „ „	£5,282,084
The Customs Revenue was	£731,883
General Revenue, ordinary and territorial	£1,299,371
The General Government Debt was	£5,493,316
Of the Banks, total Capital paid up	£4,281,529 16*s.* 6*d.*
Postal Revenue was	£70,249 19*s.* 7*d.*

The first telegraph was established under the direction of Colonel Gamble, C.B., Deputy Quartermaster-General, in 1863, and was exceedingly well worked by Lieut. Burton, Deputy Assistant Quartermaster-General, and his assistants, Corporal Brodie, R.E., and 2nd Corporal

Butcher, R.E. In December, 1871, the telegraph stations numbered seventy-one, and the number of miles of lines was 2,015.

Criminal Statistics.—The convictions in 1871 were 11,806, but many of the convictions were for drunkenness (4,751), and not for serious offences.

Meteorology.—At Wellington, the capital, Cook's Straits, in the cold month of May, mean temperature, 64°; in the hot month of December, 72°. No extremes of heat or cold, and showing the excellence of the climate. Rainfall, 64 inches; and at Auckland, 47 inches. Snow at Dunedin, 4 inches.

II.

NUMERICAL RETURN showing the Officers, Non-commissioned Officers, and Men of the various Corps serving in NEW ZEALAND killed, wounded, and died of wounds in engagements with, or ambuscade of, the insurgent Maoris, from 1st January, 1863, to 15th February, 1866.

Corps.	Killed.		Wounded.		Died of Wounds.		Total Deaths from Wounds in Action.
	Officers.	Non-commissioned Officers and Men.	Officers.	Non-commissioned Officers and Men.	Officers.	Non-commissioned Officers and Men.	
Royal Engineers	..	1	1	2	..	1	2
,, Artillery	..	5	2	5	1	..	6
Military Train	..	1	..	1	..	..	1
1st Batt. 12th Regt.	1	5	..	24	..	2	8
2nd ,, 14th ,,	..	7	6	22	2	2	11
2nd ,, 18th ,,	..	12	1	44	1	7	20
40th Regiment	..	18	3	42	2	4	24
43rd ,,	5	17	7	43	3	6	31
50th ,,	1	16	3	28	..	1	18
57th ,,	2	12	1	36	..	4	18
65th ,,	1	20	8	49	1	4	26
68th ,,	..	5	4	41	..	4	9
70th ,,	1	8	2	16	..	..	9
Medical Staff	1	..	..	..	..	..	1
Total Imperial Forces to 31st Dec. 1865	12	127	38	353	10	35	184
Royal Naval Brigade	3	13	7	34	1	1	18
Colonial Forces	3	15	7	30	3	4	25
Total 1st Jan. 1863 to 31st Dec. 1865	18	155	52	417	14	40	227
1866, to 15th Feb.:							
14th Regiment	..	2	2	7	..	2	4
43rd ,,	..	..	..	4	..	..	..
50th ,,	..	1	..	2	..	..	1
57th ,,	..	5	1	11	1	2	8
Colonial Forces	..	1	1	9	..	..	1
Total killed and wounded . 688							
Total	18	164	56	450	15	44	241

The Regular Troops in New Zealand were:—On 1st June, 1863 . . . 5245.
On 1st August, 1865 . . 10,047.

III.

RETURN of MAORIS killed, wounded, and prisoners, in 1863-4-5.

Engagement.	English strength.	Maoris.	Killed.	Wounded.	Prisoners.
Katikara	771	not known	28	not known	..
Keri Keri	..	..	..	..	13
Koheroa	284 (engaged)	400	40	..	..
Stone Depôt	..	..	6	..	..
Keri Keri	143	..	several	..	..
Paparoa (reconnoissance)	..	..	some	..	..
Merimeri　, ,	..	..	2	..	..
Great South Road (am-) buscade on) . . . .)	..	..	6	..	..
Pokino	..	..	1	..	..
Cameron	..	..	several	..	..
Razor Back	..	..	several	..	..
Pukekohe	..	..	12	..	..
Poutoko (ambuscade) . .	..	..	5	..	..
Galloway Redoubt . .	..	..	8	..	..
Wairoa	..	..	2	..	..
Poutoko	..	..	not known	..	..
Attack on Sergeant John-) son . . . . . .)	..	..	3	..	..
Mauku	..	..	5	..	..
Rangariri	1000	600 or 700	41	..	183
Waeari	..	..	37	..	2
Rangiawhia	..	..	12	..	12
Huerini	800	over 500	56	..	..
Kaitaki	..	..	not known	..	..
Orakau	800	450	127	..	7
Maungatautari . . .	..	..	..	..	30 (surren-dered)
Gate Pah	..	..	26		..
Te awa ote atua . .	..	..	60		..
Moutoa	..	..	50		..
Te Rangi	530	500	108		43
Manutahi	..	..	2		..
Nukumaru	600 (engaged)	600	70		..
Kakaramea	..	..	20	..	5
Opunaki	..	..	3	1	..
Warea	..	..	17	..	5
	..	..	747	1	300

From the above it appears that in the operations between the 4th of June, 1863, and 4th of August, 1865, the Maoris lost in killed at least 1,000 men, and in prisoners 300. How many were wounded is not known, but the number must have been at least five times greater than the killed. On the British side the proportion was much larger. Here we have at once over 6,000, and so a statement that there were never more than 2,000 men against the British is quite incorrect.

The killed and wounded in the Waitara campaign, or in General Chute's operations, are not given, but the numbers must have been large. There were also fights with the friendly natives, in which the insurgents had losses. 10,000 men for the Maoris is perhaps nearer the truth than 2,000 warriors.

NOTE.—It must be remembered that the troops had on nearly all occasions to attack the Maoris in selected positions strongly intrenched, the flanks *always* secure, and thus having to move on a very narrow front, no advantage could be made of superior numbers. The British states show the whole force; but when we deduct escorts, guards, sick, wounded, &c. &c., it is well known that two-thirds of the total strength is the most that can be calculated on for fighting.

IV.

Criticisms on the Services of the Military in New Zealand.

It is very unfortunate that an author and traveller of the distinguished ability of Mr. Anthony Trollope, in his work, "Australia and New Zealand," deceived by false information, speaks so slightingly of the British forces who were employed in the arduous and harassing duties of the service in New Zealand. We certainly did not expect this from our own countryman, and if he will take the trouble to read the narrative of the war from 1860 to 1866, derived from authentic sources, he may alter his sentiments on this subject.

Among other things connected with the war, he says there were 15,000 troops (that is, about 1864), and never more than 2,000 Maoris in arms against us, and that this was the proportion in all the engagements—fifteen to two —"and yet they were not subdued." Again, 10,000 are stated to be the number of the troops. These loose statements must have emanated from, or originated with, some one jealous of and disparaging the military, who were engaged in fighting the battles of the colonists, and looking for neither plunder, prize-money, nor grants of land —only endeavouring to obey orders, and to do their duty to the best of their ability, whilst "enduring hardness."

Some individuals seemed to take a pleasure, and to lose no opportunity in crying down the services of the regular troops, although the colony owed so much to them, and it was certainly from untrustworthy sources Mr. Trollope derived his information.

It is utterly impossible for any person to say how many Maoris were engaged against the troops at any given time, as the number was constantly varying. At one time, it is believed, the whole native population were ready to take part against the British, and it was for that reason that so large a reinforcement was applied for from England; and there is little doubt the natives would have risen throughout the north island had they not been deterred by the example made of the Waikatos.

As to the force under Sir Duncan Cameron, with the exception of a company of Forest Rangers, and a troop of mounted Volunteers under Colonel Nixon, who could only be used occasionally on account of the difficulty of foraging them, the regulars were the only troops that could fairly be said to be at the General's disposal for operations in the field, and of them a very considerable number were employed in the transport, commissariat, and other non-combatant departments. The local militia could only be employed within a certain radius (about 15 miles?) from their own settlements, and that only for a few days at a time. The Auckland Militia occupied certain posts in the neighbourhood of the settlement, at the beginning of the war, but took no part in the Waikato campaign. The New Plymouth Militia were an exception, and had some really hard work. As to the Waikato Militia, they arrived in successive detachments a considerable time after the war broke out; they were raised in Melbourne and Sydney, and naturally required a good deal of training before they could be fit to act against the Maoris. A good many were employed in the transport, and when the campaign was over the greater part were gradually paid off.

With regard to the comparative strength of the Maoris and the troops, when it is considered that the Maoris occupied the interior of the north island, about as large as England, and could, under cover of the bush, assemble unknown to the troops, and come down at any moment in force upon any one of the settlements, which were all on or near the coast, it is not surprising that a considerable force was necessary, for the double object of protecting those settlements and, at the same time, carrying on operations into the interior; but of course a stranger to the colony cannot be expected to enter into all these matters.

Where the iron heel of war treads it is truly said, " Le pays était avant sa venue comme le jardin d'Héden; et après qu'il sera parti il sera comme un désert désolé;" so we now trust that the fertile soil of New Zealand will smile with abundant harvests under both British and native cultivators, "the cattle on a thousand hills" be seen, and the glorious evergreen forests of the beautiful kauri pine, the noble rata, rimu and totara trees shading the palm-like tree fern, and nikau will contain no lurking foe—commerce flourishing, *peace* and plenty prevailing.

For the enterprising Pathfinder we would recommend an exploration and survey of sixty square miles, between Poverty Bay and the Bay of Plenty; for in preparing the map for this work from a large one of New Zealand, we found a perfect blank in that region; and here may be observed scenes of great interest, good pasture land, hot springs, and if not the living moa, the bones of that gigantic bird, the great *Dinornis elephantopus.*

V.

ACCOUNT OF THE ESCAPE OF FIFTY PRISONERS IN WELLINGTON HARBOUR, NEW ZEALAND.

THE escape of fifty Maori prisoners, on the 20th January, 1866, confined in a vessel in Wellington Harbour, may be here related as a very peculiar " incident" of the Maori war, and as it showed great daring and astuteness.

They had been taken at the time the Wereroa pah fell, and were placed on board a timber ship called the Manukau. The vessel had large bow ports, as is usual with timber ships, by which to pass in their freight. The ports had not been used for some time, and were supposed to be securely fastened.

By order of the Governor, the escort (50th Regiment) placed the prisoners on board the Manukau, and remained to guard them; but the vessel did not seem to be in a very fit state for the reception of the prisoners; the deck was lumbered with miscellaneous articles, as pieces of iron, marling-spikes, &c., some of which were thrown into the hold where the prisoners were located, immediately over a quantity of stone ballast, &c. The prisoners were always kept below at night, a sentry being on deck over the hatch.

There was a report some months before the escape that the prisoners meditated an attempt by the bow ports, but the mate of the ship, who lived on board, and the officer in command at the time, did not think that they could possibly effect it.

On the 20th of January, when it was blowing a gale of wind, a heavy sea running, and the night pitch dark, the

Maoris managed, with the assistance of a screw-key, which they got hold of among the things in the hold, to open one of the bow ports, and before daylight the following morning all but three had gone.

The darkness of the night, and the noise of the wind and sea, prevented the sentry on deck observing or hearing anything; and so cunningly did they effect their object that while the whole arrangement was going on below a single Maori occasionally came up during the night (as they were permitted to do, " to go to the head ") to divert the sentry's attention.

Three or four were drowned in trying to swim ashore, about three-fourths of a mile; two or three, when pressed by hunger, came back; one or two were shot by parties sent out in pursuit; but the great majority were not again seen.

A court of inquiry assembled to investigate the case, and the Major-General (Chute) was satisfied that no blame rested on the detachment, as the escape was made under circumstances beyond their control.

The officer was unfortunately on shore at the time, and proved that he tried to get off, but no boatman would take him. He was censured, however, for not going off earlier, when indications of boisterous weather first appeared.

The escape of the Maori leader, Te Kooti, banished with 300 others to the Chatham Islands, their seizing a schooner, and return to New Zealand, and the harassing pursuits after him, was also a remarkable event in the history of this intelligent race.

VI.

The "Duval-MacNaughton Rifle:" a new Weapon.

In Abyssinia, when the gate of the fortress of Magdala was attacked by the British troops, the garrison did not consider it fair fighting, for the rifles were fired through the loopholes at the defenders of the gate, and repeatedly fired without being withdrawn to load—they were breech-loaders.

A superior breechloader in modern warfare is of the highest importance for arming troops; and, since the introduction of the Snider rifle, a number of rival arms have been offered for the acceptance of the military authorities. We have seen the chassepot used on the Continent: the fault of it seemed its length of range, for young troops armed with it are tempted, unless under very strict discipline, to open fire at 1500 yards or more; whereas the needle-gun, with shorter range, induces those carrying it to reserve their fire for closer quarters, and with more deadly effect. As an old member of the Montreal Rifle Club, we never thought of firing over the ice of the St. Lawrence with a range of a mile, or when a man appears the size of a black pin, but preferred a much shorter range for our practice.

A very enterprising gentleman of Montreal (a relative), Mr. Edward Alexander Prentice, brought to my notice lately a new rifle with various excellencies in its construction and action; its history and description are as follows:

It was invented by an ingenious French Canadian of the name of Joseph Duval, of Laprairie, opposite to Mon-

treal. He not only made the "stock, lock, and barrel,"
but he made his own tools. Of course it was at first
rather a rough, ungainly weapon, but Mr. Prentice, recog-
nising its originality and great merit, purchased the
patent rights, with a few friends, had it well made and
much improved by Mr. James Macnaughton, gun-maker
Edinburgh; also it was superintended by Mr. Alex.
Duncan, Advocate, New Club, Edinburgh.

It was then submitted to the Minister of Militia,
Canada, Sir George E. Cartier, Bart., who ordered Lieut.-
Colonel G. A. Trench, Inspector of Artillery and Warlike
Stores, and Lieut.-Colonel M. W. Strange, R.A., Quebec, to
report on it. These gentlemen made elaborate reports, the
gist of which was that they considered it a more suitable
arm for the service of troops than the Martini rifle.

Description of the " Duval-MacNaughton " Rifle.

Barrel.—Is made of steel, ·450 bore, and rifled with seven
segmental grooves having a spiral of one turn in twenty-
one inches. The grooves are recommended to be made as
shallow as they can be made compatible with distinctness;
also that they should not touch on each other at the
edges, but that a small strip of the barrel (or land)
should be left between the grooves, say $\frac{1}{14}$ inch. broad,
which acts as an effectual check on any irregularity in
rifling.

Breech Shoe.—Is made of a mild steel, and in one piece :
it has a gap on the top (as in the "Martini"), in which the
breech block works, and also one on the right side through
which the parts forming lock and action are inserted; the
latter gap is closed by a plate which is securely held in

place by one screw. The shoe is fastened to the stock by two solid straps above and below the small.

Action.—The parts composing the action are cock or tumbler, swivel, piston, sliding tumbler, extractor, breech block, trigger, mainspring, trigger spring, and five nails. Instead of the various parts pivoting on nails as usual, they pivot on solid pillars or pivots.

Stock.—Has a jag for cleaning screwed into butt; otherwise as usual.

Advantages claimed for the " Duval-MacNaughton" Rifle.— In claiming advantages for the "Duval-MacNaughton" Rifle we must necessarily draw a comparison with some other weapon on a similar system, and one the merits of which are widely known. Let us, therefore, take for comparison the "Martini-Henry," it being well known and having been selected from a number of competitors as the future rifle of the British army. The advantages of the "Duval-MacNaughton" over the "Martini-Henry" are considered to be as follows, viz. :

Simplicity and cheapness in Manufacture.—The rifle can be machine-made throughout and thoroughly interchangeable. The parts composing the action are strong, simple, and few.

Facility for cleaning and inspecting from the rear.—This is effected by having the breech block hung on the points of two screws, and a deep groove cut through the hinge or knuckle of block; thus cleaning from the rear, we avoid the risk of allowing the fouling to get down in front of block as in the Martini-Henry, Snider, &c., and about extractors, these being placed in a rifle where dirt can least be tolerated, and where it will most readily interfere with the free working of the action.

Mainspring.—Instead of the spiral spring as used in the

Y

"Martini-Henry," and which is very generally condemned by practical men, there is retained the trusted and time-honoured V-spring nearly as used in a common lock.

Pull off.—The fickle pull off in the "Martini-Henry" is considered one of its greatest faults, and until now has defied remedy. In the new rifle, again, the old principle of tumbler and scear is adhered to, with the result of a perfectly equal and agreeable pull off.

Extracting power.—Is an accelerating motion, beginning with a strong, slow leverage to start the cartridge case, and finishing with a jerk; the power being so nicely balanced that the operator at pleasure can land the cartridge on the block just clear of the barrel, or pitch it clear over the elbow.

The facility with which this rifle can be taken to pieces and cleaned, or can be opened for cleaning, and at the same time be quite ready for use in case of surprise.—Although we read in the report of the late "Small Arms Committee" that the "Martini-Henry" may be taken to pieces and put together again by any intelligent soldier in a few minutes, we hear that in practice this is very far from being the case, but that considerable difficulty is experienced in putting together the rifle after having taken it separate. The present rifle, on the other hand, may be opened for cleaning and UNDERSTOOD by any soldier in one minute, and at the same time (when open) is quite good for firing, which, we believe, is quite a novel feature in rifles.

Piston.—Is of one piece, strong and simply made, and requires no piston spring, the first movement of the cock upward withdrawing it within the block. In the "Martini-Henry" a frequent complaint is made of the piston breaking, or getting staved up in consequence of its having to take the full blow of the mainspring when snapping the rifle without a cartridge case. In this rifle we have a large, flat surface on the front of cock striking against a similar surface on body, and together making a most excellent snapping face, and one which may be used without detriment to the arm.

Rapidity.—There being one motion less required in loading and firing the "Duval-MacNaughton" than the "Martini," it is obvious that a greater number of shots may be fired in the same time.

The "Duval-MacNaughton" rifle having a visible cock—which also acts as lever—is considered to be a great advantage, as any one may tell at a glance whether the rifle is at low, half, or full-cock; it also enables the operator to lower the lock from full-cock to half-cock, as in an ordinary rifle lock.

A second pattern of this rifle is made with an additional tumbler, which is actuated by the cock, and makes it possible to fire with the breech open or shut at pleasure.

The best method of manipulating the "Duval-Mac-Naughton" rifle is to hold it at the position of "ready," place the palm of right hand on the cock, the fingers to the right side underneath the rifle, with thumb to left side; squeeze the hand sharply together; this opens the breech, ejects the spent cartridge case, and leaves the rifle at full-cock ready for loading.

The lever by which the breech is opened being above the small or handle of the stock can easily be grasped by the right hand without relinquishing the hold on the rifle, a feature which adapts it for cavalry, with whom the left hand is fully engaged with the reins.

J. MacNaughton.

Objections to the " Martini," by an eminent Gunmaker.

1st. Dangerous from being necessarily always at cock when loaded, and giving no indication that it is so.   Is raised to cock without thought on part of the user, and yet depends for safety on his unceasing vigilance and care; being a self-cocking gun it does not provide a self-acting safety.   It is also dangerous from the uncertainty of the pull, which is sometimes so light that the least pressure on the trigger, or jar of the gun, will send it off.

2nd. Its inferior lock.   The lock of an ordinary gun has been so perfected that friction is almost absent.   Its elastic mainspring is finely-proportioned to bear the strain equally on all its parts and hung on the plate, so as to be entirely free from it in working, and so connected with the tumbler that its force is greatest when striking the blow, and least when for the purpose of the pull it should be.   In the Martini this is all reversed.   Its simple spiral spring is coiled round the strikes, causing a grating friction on every coil, and is so connected with tumbler that its least force is exerted when, for the purpose of ignition, it should be greatest, and *vice versâ*, when for the sake of the pull it should be least.

The spring of an ordinary gun exerts a pressure of 16 lbs. when down, and only 10 lbs. when up, whilst that of the Martini has a pressure of 20 lbs. when down, and 30 lbs. when up.   This great weight and friction is unnoticed from the great length of lever used, but the effect on the pull still remains, making it impossible to give the scear a firm hold in bent, and so causing the pull to wear out faster.   Again, in an ordinary gun lock raising the cock brings up the spring and tumbler, and allows the scear to drop into the bent and remain there till removed by a pull of the trigger. But this is not so with the Martini, as the scear is dropped into the bent when spring is only partly back, and is required to supply the necessary resistance to force the excessive spring the remaining distance. This contrivance is one great cause of its irregular pull, the pull being lighter or heavier according to the force and manner of closing the lever; and then how it must injure the form of the scear and bent, especially when either of them are softer in temper than they should be, and certain to break them if too hard.

The introduction of a new limb called a tumbler rest (what else is the scear) is an acknowledgment by the makers of the weakness of this part of their gun. But this additional limb is no improvement, as, although it may save the scear from breaking, it further decreases the firmness of the pull, rendering the attainment of the pull still more difficult. For example, say a pull of 6 lbs. is required, with the ordinary gun you have one bent and one scear to adjust so as to give the requisite weight. But with this new invention you have practically three scears and three bents to adjust, so that they act in unison and have the weight fairly distributed amongst them. To sum up, the power to make the pull of the Martini good is diminished one-third by the absence of the ordinary trigger, and still further by the excessive weight of the spring at cock; and then what chance remains of making it has to be divided by three, and this excessively weak pull is expected to hold its own, not only whilst sustaining the weight of the spring at cock, but whilst that spring is violently forced against it.

3rd. It recoils more than the ordinary gun, and this is due to the form of what is called the shoe, which has been constructed without studying the amount of strain it would have to bear. It is open top and bottom, its sides consisting simply of two thin plates (⅛ inch), necessarily placed wide from centre of charge and weakened by their great length (3 inches).

It is impossible for good shooting to be made with an irregular pull and excessive recoil.

Armourer-Sergeant Smiles, Grenadier Guards, stated to Lieut.-General the Hon. Sir James Lindsey, K.C.M.G., in presence of Colonel Bridges, G.G., and Mr. Prentice, that the mechanism of the Duval-MacNaughton rifle was so simple he could repair any piece in the field if it broke, which he said was not likely, as the different parts were so strong and simple that any village blacksmith can make or mend them.

The Canadian Government, having now a well-organised militia system, deem it advisable to manufacture their arms and ammunition in the country, instead of drawing supplies from England, which, in time of necessity, might be dangerous and impracticable; and with this view, not deeming the Martini a superior but an inferior weapon, several influential men in Canada have urged on the Government there the advisibility of making their own Canadian rifle—the Duval—at Montreal, or elsewhere in the Dominion; and Mr. Prentice came to England and was engaged with the Colonial and War Offices in order to get practical trials made in camp at Aldershot, &c., to justify the Canadian Government in adopting the new arm.

J. E. A.

THE END.

Lightning Source UK Ltd.
Milton Keynes UK
UKHW022237100920
369698UK00005B/169